J.M. Campen. 10/2005

# SHEPHERDS OF SUSSEX

*By the same Author*
BYPATHS IN DOWNLAND
DOWNLAND TREASURE
ETC.

*Photo by the Author*

## NELSON COPPARD

# SHEPHERDS OF SUSSEX

*By*

BARCLAY WILLS

*Foreword by*
HIS GRACE THE DUKE OF NORFOLK
E.M., K.G.

LONDON
SKEFFINGTON & SON, LTD.
PATERNOSTER HOUSE, ST. PAUL'S, E.C.4

This edition published 2001 by:
Country Books
Courtyard Cottage, Little Longstone, Bakewell
Derbyshire DE45 1NN

*A full catalogue of books in print
is available upon request from the publisher.*

ISBN 1 898941 67 X

DEDICATED TO
NELSON COPPARD,
THE FIRST SHEPHERD
I MET IN SUSSEX

# FOREWORD
# TO THE FACSIMILE EDITION

This is one of the 'classics' of Sussex books. The author, Barclay Wills, although not born in the county, grew to love both it and its characters. Here he records what was a vanishing way of life – now completely gone. The wearing of the smock or 'round frock' had already ceased, and today, were you lucky enough to find one, it would cost several hundred pounds. The life of the Downland shepherd would have been extremely lonely, living in his van on the Downs with nothing for company except his dog. Few would contemplate such an occupation today. We are fortunate that authors like Barclay Wills recorded so much of what has now been lost. The value of this reprint is that it was written from first-hand accounts – not a historian's view of what he thought it was like!

I commend it to all lovers of Sussex.

Dick Richardson
Publisher

# FOREWORD

THE author has been kind enough to ask me to write a Foreword to his new book *Shepherds of Sussex*.

I cannot do justice to his work, but as a lover of the Downs, and because it was due to the connection of Blackpatch and the original Shepherds of the Downs that this book has been written, I add a few lines.

Mr. Barclay Wills has traced the Shepherd of Sussex from the Neolithic Age to the present day, and as Blackpatch forms part of my estates, it adds a special interest.

Many countries and even counties have their own peculiar type of living man, but the Shepherd of Sussex is, perhaps we may say, a race unto himself. As Mr. Wills says in the first chapter, many books have been written about Sussex, but surely no history of the county can be complete without reference to the man that really is Sussex. It is sad to-day to see a race that will soon be gone. At my age I am too young to remember the old type of shepherd minding his flock, but to a smaller extent he is still there, and I have learned enough to know what his passing means.

In this book Mr. Wills tells of famous shepherds leading their lonely life, but nevertheless a life which to-day would be most peaceful alone with the birds and the flowers and the beasts of nature. It is a work which cannot fail to interest not only people of Sussex but those who have not the good fortune to know the Downs.

The Shepherd of Sussex might pass along his way, but it is for us who follow to see that his happy hunting ground shall be for ever left open against the day of his return.

*Norfolk.*

# CONTENTS

|  | PAGE |
|---|---|
| THE OPENING CHAPTER | 15 |
| THE HILL-SHEPHERD | 19 |
| THE LURE OF THE SHEPHERD'S WORK | 21 |
| A CHARACTER STUDY OF SUSSEX SHEPHERDS | 26 |
| THE FIRST SHEPHERDS OF SUSSEX | 30 |
| SHEPHERDS OF BYGONE DAYS | 37 |
| SOME TYPICAL SHEPHERDS | 54 |
| STRAY MEMORIES. *By Dr. Habberton Lulham* | 97 |
| THE SHEPHERD'S POSSESSIONS | 107 |
| SHEEP-CROOKS AND SHEEP-BELLS | 126 |
| SHEARING, ETC. | 154 |
| SHEEP-WASHING, MARKING AND COUNTING | 168 |
| DEW-PONDS, AND OTHERS | 176 |
| THE SHEPHERD'S COMPANION | 180 |
| THE ODD CHAPTER | 185 |
| SHEPHERDS OF THE MARSHES | 208 |
| SUSSEX SHEEP | 213 |
| THE CROW-SCARER | 239 |
| AN OLD SHEPHERD'S OPINION | 242 |
| THE END OF THE BOOK | 246 |

# LIST OF ILLUSTRATIONS

| | |
|---|---|
| NELSON COPPARD | *Frontispiece* |
| | FACING PAGE |
| THE HILL SHEPHERD | 32 |
| JAW-BONE OF SHEEP FROM EXCAVATION | 33 |
| "OFF TO THE HILLS" | 48 |
| JIM FOWLER | 49 |
| "THE CHANGELING" | 64 |
| THE SHEPHERD'S UMBRELLA | 65 |
| "A HUNDRED YEARS AGO" | 80 |
| SHEEP-CROOKS | 81 |
| SHEEP-BELLS | 112 |
| LOCKYERS | 113 |
| SHEARING GANG AT WORK | 128 |
| THE TAR BOY | 129 |
| HORN LANTERNS | 129 |
| THE SHEEP-WASH | 144 |
| SHEPHERD AND FLOCK AT POND | 145 |
| JOHN BEECHER | 160 |
| SHEPHERD NEWELL | 160 |
| "BREAK 'EM IN YOUNG!" | 161 |
| THE ROLLER-WATTLE | 192 |

## LIST OF ILLUSTRATIONS

|  | FACING PAGE |
|---|---|
| SHEEP IN DISTRESS | 192 |
| WALTER WOOLER IN SMOCK | 193 |
| MICHAEL BLANN | 193 |
| MICHAEL BLANN'S WHISTLE AND SONG BOOK | 208 |
| TOM GODDEN | 209 |
| A LAMBING-HOOK | 224 |
| TOM WRATTEN USING LAMBING-HOOK | 224 |
| BERT LINKHORN | 225 |

# AUTHOR'S NOTE

SO many books about Sussex have been written that lovers of the county must wonder whether there is room for another. The choice of subject is the excuse for this one. When first I wrote about shepherds and sheep-bells interest in them was awakened and pictures of shepherds and sheep have become popular. Many people will welcome a book, devoted entirely to shepherds, which reveals the many aspects of their lives and the romance of their craft, and will appreciate items which link the men of to-day with prehistoric shepherds who tended their flocks on the Sussex Downs thousands of years ago.

The book is the result of years of personal investigation and countless rambles in downland, and readers will forgive the frequent use of "first person, singular," as they turn the pages and realize that only my love for the subject prompted the making of such a true and detailed record.

My thanks are due to all who have assisted me with information, gifts, and loans of specimens, also to Dr. Habberton Lulham for his contributions, and to various publishers for permissions to print extracts, and last, but not least, to Mr. Loader of Worthing for the careful preparation of many enlargements of my "Brownie" snaps used as illustrations.

B. W.

WORTHING

# SHEPHERDS OF SUSSEX

## THE OPENING CHAPTER

UNTIL this book was compiled no history of the shepherds of Sussex had been written, although the fame of Sussex sheep is world-wide. The sheep had received their share of attention, and interesting accounts of old flockmasters had been recorded, but the poor shepherds, whose untiring devotion to the sheep resulted in the renown of the flockmasters, lacked an historian until it was almost too late to gather the necessary information for the purpose.

That the time was more than ripe for noting such items as are contained in the various chapters is proved by the fact that while some of these were appearing as articles in the *Sussex County Magazine* a number of the oldest hill-shepherds, who had looked forward to reading this book, passed away. I had predicted the fading out of the old men, but it started sooner than I expected, so that although the book was begun as an up-to-date record it has already become the history of a race that has almost disappeared.

In *Downland Treasure* I affirmed that such a book as this was really a task for someone with more money and leisure than myself, but eventually I was persuaded to undertake it. Fortunately my many rambles to see shepherds, when collecting sheep-bells, had paved the way for further enquiries, but when planning the chapters I realized that much of the success in obtaining the information I wanted would depend on the attitude of the shepherds, and I resolved to consult one of them first. Nelson Coppard can be trusted to express his opinion without hesitation, and as we sat on an old machine-frame beside a barn and discussed the various ways of recording details remembered by shepherds he showed a preference for a series of accounts of actual interviews.

"We will begin now," said Nelson, in his quaint direct way; " you ask me what you want to know, an' I'll tell you all I can, an' you put it down : then, if 't seems all right, you can do t' same to t' next one ! " Between us we arranged the principal points for enquiry and subsequently I found that his idea appealed equally to other men I visited. They welcomed the plan of a book devoted to themselves and their craft, and responded willingly to requests for details of their lives and information on many subjects. Family treasures were unearthed; old days were remembered again; names and places were quoted, and I was able to follow many trails which resulted in the gathering of valuable facts regarding former habits that had been almost forgotten under the stress of modern ways in sheep-farming.

Naturally there were little disappointments incidental to such a quest, such as journeys to see aged people whose recollections were too vague to be of any real use, and tales of specimens thrown away as useless before I arrived, but these were more than balanced by sudden surprising kindness from many people, by new friendships, and by joyous hours when unexpected discoveries were made. Now the book is finished I count it a privilege that it fell to my lot to act as historian for these men of simple nature and many virtues, and if my records lead to appreciation and kindly feeling for the members of a race so often overlooked, my main object will be achieved.

The interviews carry their own value, and the chapters on bells, crooks, and other things are the result of personal observation; but on certain matters I have recorded statements made by those who can speak with authority, and have used quotations which support and confirm items of information given to me by old shepherds, in order that the book may be used as a reliable work of reference on matters appertaining to shepherds' work in the county.

It is inevitable that many readers will wish that portraits of men they know could have been included, but those chosen are typical, and must represent the full number. It is also possible that, although so many enquiries have been made, there may be other details of old ways and customs that should have found a place among the rest; but, as many writers know, the gleaning of information on special subjects is not always easy. After tracking down particulars of one small matter I happened to mention it to another shepherd. "Fancy you wantin' to know *thet*!" he exclaimed—"why, I could ha' told ye, but I diddun think nothen to it!"

Enthusiasts who look for fresh and unusual items in Sussex books will appreciate the value of certain little records. The portrait of a shepherd of a hundred years ago, the whistle-pipe and song-book of Michael Blann, the shearing gang and tar-boy pictures, the notes on horn lanterns, and many odd items might have been lost for ever if the " shepherds' book," as the old men called it, had not been written.

During my rambles I acquired many souvenirs and specimens of things made and used by shepherds. It seemed fitting that these treasured possessions of various men should all find a home together, and they are now in Worthing Museum, where Miss Gerard, the Curator, has arranged a "shepherds' collection" as a special exhibit for those who are interested in the bygones of the county.

## THE HILL-SHEPHERD

'TIS good to tramp the downs and meet
A grazing flock, to hear the sweet
Soft chimes from canisters that swing
Above the turf; The songs they sing
Delight the shepherd as he stands,
With crook-head clasped between his hands
And stick-end pressed into the grass,
While he surveys the sheep that pass.
'Tis good to see him on the hill,
To ponder on the joys that fill
Some little part of his long hours
In company of sheep and flowers,
For he is of an ancient race
Of men, who love free open space,
The sun, and wind, and sky, and all
The out-door world, whose beauties call
So oft in vain.  His actions tell
That sheep have cast a curious spell
Upon him, and a bleating cry
Acts as a charm;—the reason why
He may not think about, nor know,
But he responds,—and he will go,
As long as strength permits, to see
His helpless woolly family :
And satisfied with simple joy
Will precious leisure time employ
In listening to a favourite bell
Whose company he loves so well;

For as the music drifts along
He finds allurement in its song;
"*Hark to 'un now!*" he said to me,—
"*Thet be a good 'un, thet bell be!*"

B. W.

# THE LURE OF THE SHEPHERD'S WORK

WHEN the blackberry harvest draws people from the towns the shepherd's territory is often invaded by folk who go to pick in the same spot each season. It is their annual excuse for a " day out," their one opportunity to experience that sense of freedom which only the country-side can offer. Unconsciously they note the presence of rooks and other birds, of butterflies, of cattle, or a flock of sheep. A casual glance may reveal the shepherd, with his dog in attendance.

" There's that old shepherd again ! " I heard one woman say to another, " still standing about ! He looks just the same as when we came last year ! " So he may do ! So do the rooks, the butterflies, and the cattle; so do the brambles and the familiar view around, and though the berry-pickers are a year older, and must have done a certain amount of work during the year, they are apt to forget that the shepherd has any hard work at all. He may look " just the same " as when they came last year, but few realize what he has done in the interval. Lambing time, when he was on duty day and night, has passed again, with all its usual round of labour and anxiety. Other jobs have followed: tailing, cutting, shearing, dipping, and trimming. Day by day, in all sorts of weather, he has tended his flock. (What a multitude of duties are included in the word " tended " —you cannot realize it unless you have been in his company constantly.) Now he stands, apparently idle, but it is safe to assert that his thoughts are centred on the ewes, for on his care of them during the winter months depends the success of next lambing time.

So each year passes, and the shepherd carries on, working seven days a week. In return for such devotion he receives a wage which other workers would despise. I have known a farmer to say : " I wouldn't part with old Mike ; no matter when I go by, early or late, weekday or Sunday, he is always about, looking after the sheep !" Perhaps he imagined that old Mike worked simply to please him, but it was not so. Such work is not all done for the sake of the farmer, for if the shepherd moved to another farm he would do just the same. It is the lure of his craft which causes him to put his dumb families before everything else, and to stay with them for many an extra hour in order to give a " last look round," for their benefit.

Many references have been made in print to the lives of shepherds, and many opinions expressed concerning their outlook on life. If we were able to interview all the old Sussex shepherds at this date we should probably find that the majority of them view the changes and ways of modern times with a certain amount of disfavour. They are forced to adapt themselves to new conditions and move with the times to some extent, but the habits of a lifetime (in many cases strengthened by hereditary tendencies) are not easily altered.

My hours spent with shepherds at all seasons of the year have been a revelation in many ways. My own early idea of a shepherd, as a man, crook in hand, with nothing to do but to watch his flock, was soon exploded. Gradually I sorted out the many little tangled lines of thought that occurred to me ; gradually I traced the reason for some action or for the careful attention given to some little detail, and every fact I gleaned pointed backwards—back through the years to the days when the shepherd learned his craft, and sometimes further still, to the time of his parents and grandparents. One old man explained a point thus : " My gran'father did it thet way, an' my father did it thet way, an' now *I* doos it the same. There be a right way an' a wrong way o' doin' things, an' the sooner you learns to do a thing the right way the better it be for ye, for then yew see yew doos it right wi'out thinkin' 'bout it."

Many of the oldest shepherds now living started work at a very early age. They absorbed the details of their craft at a date when the craze for speed was unknown; when, as one old man remarked to me, " the farmer shared the shepherd's pride and delight in the flock, and in all the shepherd did." That is why we still find old men doing more than a young man would expect to do for the wages paid. With experience of duties gained as shepherd boy, teg boy, and under-shepherd grew that pride which was shared by the farmer—a pride which even extended to the bells used on the flock.

How different it is to-day ! The craze for speed has affected everybody. Ways have changed ; good manners are old-fashioned ; thoroughness is out of date ; the old shepherd himself is out of date ; few care twopence about his thoroughness or his pride in work ; his only enjoyment is in the thought of past days when he was " somebody," and so any old shepherd you meet is usually quiet and reticent until he discovers whether your interest is genuine. If he is satisfied you soon know ; he responds to enquiries, but he is like a dormouse waking up in spring, for at the touch of memory's hand his attitude changes, his stiffness relaxes, his eyes are young again, and as he talks for a little while he becomes " somebody " once more !

Do not despise an old shepherd because he appears to be simple ; his simplicity is actually a sign of strength. He may not fit in with modern ideas, but it must be remembered that when he started with an inborn love for one kind of work he was first taught obedience, correctness, thoroughness, self-reliance, and untiring devotion to the flock. As shepherd he became a man of importance and ruled his own little kingdom. The drawbacks attending his job were the long hours, the many inconveniences resulting from unkind weather, and the low wages; but there were compensations in other ways. His rather hard upbringing helped him to tackle every task in a methodical manner, without unnecessary worry, and his solitary peaceful hours in the open air gradually cast a spell over him—a spell so strong that at last he developed this quiet, simple manner. Hidden under this cloak is a wonderful love for the freedom of open spaces, for pictures of sheep on the hillside and in the fold, for fields of mangold and rape, for the familiar starlings and the hundred and one items which he meets and notes as he goes to and fro.

Dog, crook, and favourite bells are still his principal possessions. His pleasure is in his flock, and, happy in the many memories of past days, he jogs on, impatient with new farmers, with alterations in farming methods, and with golfers and motorists who invade his once quiet grazing grounds. Gone are the old sheep-shearing suppers in which he took part,—gone are the old songs in which he joined,—gone is the farmer who was human enough to compliment him on the chimes from his old sheep-bells. Gone, too, are many other shepherds who were his friends when he was young. They have passed away, and he admits that he is one of a dying race, but in spite of all this he carries on his usual daily work with the same unwavering persistence—especially if he be a man from a family of hill-shepherds.

The term "shepherd" embraces those who tend flocks on the hills, on flat farms, and on the marshes. At one time I thought that the hill-shepherds considered themselves a peg above the others, because some had owned that they would never leave the hills to look after a " farm flock," but when I had been in their company a hundred times, at every season of the year, I understood why the lives of these old-fashioned men are filled with romance, although they do not appear to be aware of it, and why a " farm flock " would not satisfy them.

Stand with an old shepherd on a hill-top on a fine summer day, and you will capture some of the beauty which has moulded his character and that of his ancestors. He is king of a beautiful and peaceful little kingdom. The purest breezes caress him. The music of his precious sheep-bells delights him. As he looks across to other hills and into the valleys and watches the sun chase the cloud-shadows over the turf he may tell you, in a simple manner, that in the same way a fine day on the hill-top chases away remembrances of hours of work in bad weather. He may tell you of bygone days when he caught glimpses of other shepherd friends on distant hills and how the wind brought the sound of other bells to him. The flower-studded turf and the wild life around are more to him than any book could be. You may count the varieties of blossoms and name them all, but names out of books mean very little to the shepherd. All the flowers are friends that he has known from his earliest years. There are moments when you feel that his love for the hill-tops is beyond description in words, and, in a vague way, that such a man is superior to the ordinary mortal whose life is full of trivial affairs. He has partaken of the peace of height and expanse, the beauty of sunrise and sunset, the company of birds and flowers and grass, and generations of sheep for so long that his whole outlook on life is far above your own. The poor old hill-shepherd may have given lifelong work for a meagre wage, but he is rich in many things that money cannot buy!

## A CHARACTER STUDY OF SUSSEX SHEPHERDS

THE characters of Sussex shepherds are so complex that consideration of some facts is necessary before they can be properly understood. We may discover that many of them are unlettered, or that some are blessed with more humour than others, but such points are of minor importance. The main factors responsible for their characters are hereditary traits and environments, and when all points are considered we find the reasons for the strangely similar characteristics found in most of the men when studied individually.

Among all the old Sussex ways there were few so important in its far-reaching effects as smuggling, and the many recorded facts are sufficient to prove that all classes were more or less affected by it. Whether the part taken by any individual was active or passive the need for secrecy and silence was the same, and in course of time the pose adopted by those interested would naturally tend to become, not only a family trait but a strong factor in the forming of Sussex character. Here we have a possible explanation of that peculiar reserve noticeable in many Sussex people.

The apparent absence of motive is very strange and very tiring to those from other counties who know of no reason for it, and was responsible for a remark made to me : " Some people here are afflicted with spasms in their likes and dislikes ; sometimes they seem to like you, and sometimes they don't. You must never be surprised at anything they do, or don't do; and don't ever worry about it, because it isn't worth while!" Strangers to the county have many opportunities to reflect on the temperament of certain people who do not respond to advances, who will promise and not perform, who will refuse for no reason at all to do a job for someone who is willing to pay a good price, or who will refuse for some obscure reason to answer a simple question, and say, afterwards, " I wasn't going to have *my* brains picked!" Strangers often say hard things in haste without stopping to consider that these " spasms " may not be a result of bad temper. They are unaware of the fact that the subtle feeling which prevents certain people being frank and honest to strangers may be an unrecognized heritage from their ancestors of the old smuggling days.

Some people are saddled with a further inheritance—a wilful and masterful disposition, which makes them very aggressive. I have heard this trait referred to as " orkardness "; to many it is a virtue—a sign of great strength of character. People put up with an " orkard " man and respect him, whereas the stranger shuns him as he would a dog with a surly temper.

Fortunately for everybody there are two distinct types of character in Sussex. We have noted the worse. The other type lacks the uncomfortable characteristics, and though there may be a certain amount of caution in their disposition it is tempered with more humour and a greater tendency to friendliness. This mixture of two types is bewildering to a " foreigner," as is the fact that although in anything on a business basis he generally gets the worst of the bargain, yet, as if to make up for it, he occasionally meets people who surprise him by unexpected kindness.

So much for hereditary traits. The shepherds would doubtless conform to one type or the other except for the strong influences of environment, by the influence of which they have become as a separate race. In addition to a hard drilling in youth in careful and expert performance of duties and in pursuance of customs handed down, the old shepherds have had the charm and freedom of a life in the open air from boyhood, combined with the softening influence of constant company of dog and flock, such as no other workers experience.

By taking all these items into consideration we can at last understand more of the character of any particular man, and make due allowance for his ways and views. One man I knew (who confessed that his grandfather was a smuggler) took a long time to thaw, but casual mention of a sheep-dog brought a new light into his eyes, and pleasant interviews followed. A second has been friendly from the first minute when we met. He has a rare fund of humour, and a wonderful love of sheep and bell-music. He cannot read a book without difficulty, but can interpret the signs of the outdoor world with unerring accuracy. I could reel off a list of shepherds and their peculiarities, but it is sufficient to record that in almost every case the fascination of sheep-tending has counteracted other inborn influences to a large extent. The daily, almost hourly, task of ministering to successive helpless families has effectually ousted any tendency to lack of moral responsibility so apparent in some folk, and has increased the qualities of patience and kindness to a marked degree. This kindness is shared by the members of their families, as is proved by the cordial welcome which I have received so many times while collecting information for these records.

The lonely lives of generations of shepherds on their tracts of Downland year after year, with space, sky, and wind, with lark songs and bell-music as their daily portion, have tended to develop a simple, peaceful, philosophic frame of mind and a broad vision which may be envied by ordinary folk who are in the toils of convention.

One result of this broad outlook on life is the regard which all shepherds have for other members of the profession, and their free-and-easy ways of helping one another in various ways. That many a kindness is done within their circle is evident from some of the remarks I have heard at odd times.

"I have *another* crook, but it is lent to Dick M——. His crook broke asunder at lambing time, you see, an' I fitted he out. 'Specs he'll be sendin' it back time he gets 'nother one made."

"This beant *my* dog, you know. I lost mine las' winter. This 'un's only borrowed. She belongs to Fred B——."

"Well, you see, I can't say nothen to that, for they bells be lent to me for the winter."

"Yes, I did have some o' they bells, but I sold 'em to 'nother shepherd more'n a year ago; at least, I arn't bin *paid* for 'em yet, but they be sold all the same."

Shepherds find little real need for intercourse with the outside world, which does not understand them, but this comradeship among themselves is very strong. The hidden feelings of the man with the crook can only be thoroughly appreciated by another of his race. An attempt to summarize the characters of the old shepherds results in admiration of them. In Sussex we find old men who are simple and strong, who are so capable in their work that they are intolerant of supervision in any form, who say what they think, and do what they promise, who revel in quiet, dry humour, who help one another in times of emergency, and whose surprising kindness would often shame people who are merely upright and just. These old men have more virtues than vices; they live in a little world of their own; and as they pass out the county is losing some of its most sincere workers.

# THE FIRST SHEPHERDS OF SUSSEX

ALTHOUGH any account of shepherds and sheep in prehistoric days must necessarily be a mixture of few facts and many fancies, there is some fascination in endeavouring to piece the puzzle together.

Until we have assimilated the evidence of archæologists on the subject we cannot give rein to our fancies, but fortunately the facts recorded by the highest authorities are so clear that as we read them it becomes possible to link up the present with the past, and to imagine some of the spots we know in Sussex Downland as they appeared when the first shepherds and flocks wandered there, before the dawn of written history.

The comments of Sir Wm. Boyd Dawkins, in his book *Early Man in Britain*, sum up the known facts regarding the introduction of domestic animals into this country. He wrote:

" The sheep of the pile dwellings (Switzerland) was horned, and of a fine, delicate breed. . . . Neither of these animals (sheep and goats) is represented by any wild stock in Europe. . . . It is therefore clear that we must seek their ancestry in some other quarter of the world.

" The remains of most of these domestic animals are found in association with Neolithic implements, not merely in Britain, but in Italy, Spain, France, Germany, and Scandinavia, and imply that the same breeds were kept by the herdsmen of that remote age over the greater part of the Continent. It is, however, interesting to note that the local varieties presented now by our domestic breeds, and produced by long continued selection, have not been observed, up to this time, in Neolithic Europe.

"It is a remarkable fact that the domestic animals appear to have been introduced into Europe *en masse*, and not, as they might have been expected, one after another. The turf hog, the Celtic shorthorn, the sheep, and the goat must have been domesticated in the countries in which their wild ancestors were captured—by the hunter in Central Asia. . . . It is therefore probable that all the domestic animals came into Europe with their masters from the south-east—from the Central Plateau of Asia, the ancient home of all the present European peoples. This conclusion is confirmed by examination of the Neolithic cultivated seeds and fruits."

In connection with the subject of Neolithic shepherds some notes included in *Men of the Old Stone Age*, by Henry Fairfield Osborn, are of great assistance in helping us to form more definite ideas, as will be seen from the following extract. In these notes, relating to the natives of the Canary Islands, the author remarks:

"Anthropologists are agreed that the natives of the archipelago, at the time of its conquest, *in the fifteenth century*, were a composite people of three races. . . . *These natives were in a Neolithic state of civilization.*"

The same author also quotes from the writings of Dr. René Verneau, who resided among the natives for five years. In reference to one of the races (all cave-dwellers) Dr. Verneau recounts a visit to a cabin " worthy of the Paleolithic Age," and says:

"I had no need to make any great effort to imagine myself with a descendant of those brave shepherds of earlier times. . . . The walls, which gave free access to the wind, supported a roof composed of unstripped tree trunks, covered with branches. Stones piled on top prevented the wind from tearing it off."

A visit to a shepherd's hut at Teneriffe is described. In one corner was a bed of fern. The old shepherd had a reed flute, a wooden bowl, and a goatskin sack filled with gofio (a kind of millet).

Of the old race known as the Guanchos the record states that the chiefs led a very simple life, and were no richer than the average mortal. "They did not disdain to inspect their flocks or their harvest in person."

Although the above extracts have no connection with Sussex, yet it is curious that the habits of those shepherds still living in a Neolithic state of civilization seem to link their ancestors with the old Sussex men whose reminiscences are recorded here, for they correspond in at least three ways: namely, in the use of rough huts or cabins, dry-fern bedding, and reed pipes or similar instruments; in fact, it will be found that such records of shepherds as are available, irrespective of date, indicate in small ways that many methods and customs of the generation now passing out are the result of teaching handed down from age to age.

It is possible that this is the reason why important records of past Sussex shepherds are so few. Perhaps the daily life of a shepherd, considered as an unending round of unchanging duties, caused him to become more or less overlooked. Probably like the sheep-bells, which were also overlooked, he was such a familiar feature of the countryside that he ceased to be regarded as a subject worth anything more than a casual remark.

For those interested in the county of Sussex the story

*(See p. 19)*                            *Photo by Dr. Hubberton Lulham*

# "WITH CROOK-HEAD CLASPED BETWEEN HIS HANDS"

JAW BONE OF SHEEP FROM EXCAVATION AT BLACKPATCH HILL

*Photo by: Louder, Worthing*

THE FIRST SHEPHERDS OF SUSSEX 33

is continued in the records of its archæological societies relating to excavations which have been carried out in various localities.

As such work is gradually extended, and evidence accumulates, more will be known, but the following notes from some of the official records are sufficient for the present purpose.

As in the case of remains found at The Trundle, Goodwood, and Whitehawk Camp, near Brighton, it is occasionally difficult to identify limb bones of sheep and goats owing to absence of horn cores or skull material. Fortunately discoveries in other places gave definite results.

At an Early Iron Age site at Findon Park, about a mile north of Cissbury, fragments of animal remains were discovered in pits, including those of ox, sheep, pig, deer and horse. The report states that the remains of sheep include nineteen teeth, and that no significant difference in size or otherwise could be found on comparing the teeth with those from skulls of modern sheep.

Within a few miles of Worthing are two imposing hills—Harrow and Blackpatch. Both are pitted with more or less circular hollows—the sites of ancient flint-mines—and such work as has been done has already revealed a mass of evidence of vast interest and value.

Dr. E. Cecil Curwen has kindly provided me with notes relating to the one mine opened at Harrow Hill. Bones of sheep were found in the infilling of the mine-shaft at depths of six, thirteen, sixteen, and twenty and a half feet, while in a layer of mould at the top, only twelve to eighteen inches from the datum-line, bones of oxen, deer, and sheep were discovered, those of the latter including a mandible with teeth and pieces of a horned skull.

Further work has been done on Blackpatch Hill, where more traces of sheep were discovered. Messrs.

J. H. Pull and C. H. Sainsbury kindly assisted by sending me the full report of one typical mine opened by them, and also a sheep jaw-bone, complete with teeth, which they found. In one of their published articles they say:

"Possessed of the domesticated ox, pig, and sheep, the dwellers in Downland at the time when the flint-mines were in operation must be considered as a pastoral people."

Their official report on the excavated mine contains a detailed account of fourteen layers of infilling of the shaft, summarized as follows:

*Class* 1. Contemporary debris discharged from the galleries of the shaft at the time of mining.

*Class* 2. Material mined from neighbouring shafts sunk at a later date than this and thrown into this shaft after it had fallen into disuse.

*Class* 3. Workshop and domestic debris, resulting from the use of the partly filled shaft, as a refuse pit, or as a temporary shelter for carrying on the industry of flint working.

*Class* 4. Material accumulated by natural agencies which are for ever at work upon the open hill-slopes.

The infilling of Class 3, found just below the surface soil, is thus described:

"It comprised flakes, chipped pieces, nodules, unfinished and finished implements, cooking stones, bones and teeth of animals (ox, pig, and sheep), fragments of red-deer antler, and several water-worn pebbles."

The sheep jaw-bone illustrated facing page 33 was found, with several others, when one of these mine-shafts was uncovered.

In the centre of the shaft, at the base of the surface soil, was a mass of flint-workshop debris and animal bones. The layer included a Cissbury type axe, an ovate implement, a hammer stone of liver-coloured quartzite, the usual flakes and chippings, and a number of lower jaws of sheep. This pile rested directly on the rain-wash.

The full report on the discoveries at Blackpatch has been published in a fascinating book by Mr. Pull (*The Flint Miners of Blackpatch*, Williams and Norgate, 1932), but if more than the bare facts of the excavators' reports is needed to stir the imagination, a visit to Blackpatch Hill will supply the necessary stimulant. We can there inspect the flint mines, chipping floors, and hut sites. Other similar mining centres are within easy distance, and in between them are tracts of Downland with farms in the hollows.

With the evidence of archæologists before us we may wander about these slopes, gathering impressions of the pastoral folk who lived here in the Stone Age. Their flint implements are sometimes brought to the surface by rabbits, while the removal of only an inch or two of soil, by animals or through the effects of weather, so often reveals specimens of their handiwork that we unconsciously take it for granted that we are enjoying much the same views of the hills as did those prehistoric peoples.

Oxen, pigs, and sheep were kept in those far-away ages; to-day, on the farms in the valleys, the same work is being done. Shepherds and flocks of prehistoric times used these slopes; and to-day shepherds and flocks may still be seen there.

I have already published an account of a ramble, in the course of which I discovered five live sheep in a hole on Blackpatch Hill. The last one rescued had wedged itself into a cavity which apparently communicated with a gallery of the adjacent flint mine. It was roped and hauled out. This incident happened only a few yards from the spot where the jaw bones of the small prehistoric sheep were discovered.

By such simple experiences past and present are linked up and the long interval is bridged even in daylight, but if we care to linger around till sundown, when twilight gives each hill-crest its true outline, we seem to get closer still to the ancient days. Stay until the litter of motoring parties who have desecrated this romantic place is hidden by shadows, until the ragged shapes of the juniper bushes are lost in a haze of purple gloom and loom up suddenly as we approach them. Wander along the old trackway, which covers chipping floors thousands of years old, and as the distant view fades, and shadows round us deepen we see the approach to the settlement as it must have appeared to the Stone Age folk who came home that way when their day's work was over.

The gloom deepens; the fading outlines become more blurred; we descend the slope, and, from the valley, the hill-top is but a great grey mass—the Stone Age men must have seen it thus!

Up the slope we trudge till we reach the next brow— and before we descend again we look back and picture the home of some of the first shepherds of Sussex!

# SHEPHERDS OF BYGONE DAYS

THERE are very few early records relating to Sussex shepherds, but the following are of particular interest.

In the *Sussex Archæological Collections* is a record of some letters to Ralph de Nevill, Bishop of Chichester, 1222–24, some of which refer to agricultural items in Sussex. A document relating to an enquiry into the estate of one John de Nevill revealed the fact that one of his shepherds was from Leicestershire, one from Gloucestershire, and another from Worcestershire.

Another note records that a Cistercian monk from Bordesley, co. Worcester, " has brought up lambs and sheep from the abbot, the shepherd to be left with them."

The compiler infers from these entries that there must have been a dearth of good shepherds in Sussex in the thirteenth century.

Mention of the thirteenth century leads to another item. Wool smuggling has little to do with Sussex shepherds, as far as we know, but is worth noting in connection with any study of sheep and production of wool. In the thirteenth and fourteenth centuries changes in the wool trade resulted in illicit export of much wool from the coasts of Kent and Sussex. I have found no evidence that shepherds had anything to do with this practice and no evidence to the contrary, but as the smuggling of goods into the country was carried on for centuries it is probable that many shepherds and other outdoor workers were drawn into the trade. Mr. Arthur Beckett once conversed with a shepherd in the neighbourhood of East Dean near Eastbourne who remembered sheep being driven over the tracks of a smuggling gang in order to obliterate any marks which might help the preventive officers.

I am indebted to the late Librarian and present Librarian of Worthing Public Library, Miss Marian Frost and Miss E. Gerard, for help in tracing many references to shepherds and their work, and particularly for the opportunity to quote from one old book which is in the collection.

In 1596 Leonard Mascal published his *Government of Cattel*, one section of which was devoted to sheep. The author was a member of an old family settled at Plumpton, Sussex, and although no mention of the county appears in his book on sheep some extracts are quoted here, for among his notes and instructions on the management and doctoring of sheep a few passages suggest that many of the scenes so familiar to us in these days are repetitions of those in vogue nearly three hundred and fifty years ago.

Here is a paragraph relating to sheep-pens:

". . . And also to make your Pens neere the fields or pastureside in some dry ground, and make also partitions therein to receive smal troupes of forty or more, with gates unto them, that when ye have drawne them ye may fasten each gate by himselfe, and there the shepheard may turne them, and looke if any of them be faulty in any other cause, and therein to amend them. For if his Penne be made in parts he may take and divide them at his pleasure, and when he hath taken so many as he shall thinke needfull he may turne all the rest for pasture. And those which are in the Penne he may use as he shall thinke good: this shall suffice for your Penfold."

My interview with Walter Wooler, at marking time, records this arrangement of small pens with "gates" carefully fastened when the sheep were drawn in small lots for marking.

Referring to the shepherd and his dog the author says:

"Also he must teach his dog to barke, when he would have him to run, and to run and to leave running when he would, or else he is no cunning Shepheard."

We see the result of the same careful teaching to-day. A familiar sight on the Downs is the dog, obeying a look, a movement, or muttered command, rounding up a flock and returning to the shepherd's side directly a signal is given.

Writing of trimming, which is occasionally necessary to keep sheep clean, the author gives us a little word-picture of the shepherd with his gear:

"If it then be the hot time of Summer it were good to rub (the place) over with a little tarre to keepe flies away. Also Shepheards should have a little board, by his fold side, to lay his sheepe cleane thereon when hee dresseth him, and his tar-bottle to hang ready thereby fast on a forked sticke. He should not goe without a dogge and his sheep-hooke, knife, sheeres and tar-boxe ever with him or at his fold."

This reference to the "sheep-hooke" is interesting. As noted in the later chapter on sheep-crooks in these records, the specimens made at Pyecombe in the old days were referred to as "Pyecombe hooks," and although "sheep-crook" is the favourite term now it appears that "hooke" was the usual word in 1596.

Some shepherds in these days who are used to flocks

of Southdowns resent being given other breeds to mix with them. Here is a note on mixed flocks:

"Ye must not mingle them of a strange kind with others of your flock, for those being of a strange kind they will always stand gazing about, and will rather seek to file than to feed, or else look on others."

When I read this I remembered one man who was given some Border-Leicesters by a new farmer, much to his annoyance. He soon tired of the mixed flock, and when I visited him, and enquired about them, he said: "They be over there inside the wire, an' there they stays. Damn 'em, I don' like 'em; they be more like goats than sheep. If t'boss don' soon lose 'em 'e'll lose *me!*"

Another man, looking at a pen of sheep at a sale, said to his friend: "Give I 'Downs (Southdowns), not they jumpers! I saw t'old man lookin' at 'em jus' now. 'Don' you go buyin' I any o' they jumpers,' I says, 'for they beant no good along o' my 'Downs—they kips me runnin' 'bout too much.'"

The small hut on wheels which is usually seen near sheep-folds was also known to Mascal, for in connection with folds, etc., it is recorded that "in some place the shepheard hath his Cabbin going upon a wheele for to remove here and there at his pleasure."

A study of Mascal's exhaustive essays leads one to think that the details of a shepherd's work are much the same to-day as they were in the days of Queen Elizabeth, but in one particular his book is a surprise, as the following extract shows:

"Moreover the shepheard which doth keepe them, ought to be wise in governing them with gentlenes, as it is commanded to all keepers of cattell whatsoever they be, which ought to shew themselves conductors and guiders of cattel, and not as masters, and to make them go, or to call them : they ought either to cry or to whistle, and after to shew them the sheepe-hooke, but to throw nothing at them, for that doth feare them: nor yet to stray farre off from them, nor to sit or lye downe. . . .

"There is no man that loves sheepe but will have a chiefe care of them to use and order them as they ought to be, considering all the commodities that come by them, and to keepe their houses cleane and warme in Winter, with their folds also well set and ordered in Summer. The shepherd ought to be of a good nature, wise, skilfull, countable, and right in all his doings, wherein few are to be found at this day, especially in Villages and Townes, for by their idle- nesse and long rest they grow now to waxe stubborne, and are given (for the most part) to frowardnesse and evill, more than good profit to their Masters, and ill mannered, whereof breeds many a theevish con- dition, being pickers, lyars and stealers, and runners about from place to place, with many other infinite evils. Which contrary was in the first shepherds of Egypt, and other in their time, for they were the first inventers of Astrology and judgement in starres, and finders out of Physicke, augmenters of Musicke, and many other liberall Sciences."

Like many other old books, this one is liberally besprinkled with exhortations (which were expected), but such general condemnation of shepherds is rather a shock to those acquainted with shepherds of Sussex. There is nothing to show whether Sussex shepherds ever deserved such censure, but if they did, their ways must have altered considerably during the next two hundred years, for the wonderful improvement of the South- down breed, started by John Ellman, of Glynde, could scarcely have been continued without their co-operation.

As will be seen from the interviews to be recorded here the greatest point emphasized by old shepherds to-day is the need for more of the old devotion to duty to which former generations were accustomed.

In a former book I wrote of a shepherd who prophesied the end of the old-fashioned members of his profession, and, speaking of old days, said: " 'Tis the times, you see; us old uns was poor, but things was different, an' a shepherd was *somebody* then, *but now us be nobody at all!*"

That this was no idle boast is proved by reference to the writings of Richard Lower, of Chiddingly, Sussex. In *Stray Leaves*, published in 1862, he included " a stray leaf concerning old Southdown shepherds," from which the following extracts are taken :

" The position of a shepherd at the present day (1862) is very different, especially on the South Downs, from what it was only a century back. I can speak from my personal knowledge, as for seventy years I have a distinct remembrance of a shepherd's life, and have learnt by tradition of my ancestors, at least seventy years further back, that a shepherd was then a person of no mean position. He was decidedly the chief servant, and generally from generation to generation a kind of heirloom to a farm, for whatever changes occurred the shepherd was still a fixture there. As for parting with a shepherd, Master Giles would almost as soon have thought of separating from his good old spouse.

" Then, too, the far greater number of the South Down farms were held in what was called *tenantry*, that is in small scattered divisions, greater or less, and for the general benefit of all. The sheep, though possessed by many, formed but one flock, called the *tenantry flock* ; one shepherd with his subalterns was of course sufficient to manage the flock, and was paid by his several employers in proportion to the stake each held therein. He also held a mutual interest, for his wages were chiefly in kind. In addition to his pecuniary stipend he was allowed to keep from ten to forty or fifty sheep solely for his own profit. This the farmer doubtless found to be good policy, for while the shepherd was promoting the interest of his employers, he was studying his own.

"Many of those tenantry flocks were what were called *dry* flocks, principally consisting, that is, of *wethers*. These wethers were always kept until their third or fourth year, for till they attained that age they were scarcely considered *mutton*."

*Note.*—Another reference to shepherds, written by Gilbert White in 1769, is included in the chapter on roller-wattles and sheep.

No record of Sussex shepherds would be complete without some details of two men whose names became famous in the county; namely, John Dudeney and Stephen Blackmore.

## JOHN DUDENEY, 1782–1852

In the *Sussex Archæological Society's Collections* for 1849 is a paper by Mr. R. W. Blencowe concerning Sussex shepherds. The chapter contains a long account of John Dudeney, the famous shepherd, who became a schoolmaster.

Mr. Blencowe's introduction is as follows:

"To Mr. John Dudeney, of Lewes, the descendant from a long line of shepherds, I am indebted for all the information I have received on the subject of this paper. Having begun life as a shepherd boy, he is now, at an advanced age, engaged in a different but kindred pursuit, that of schoolmaster, attending kindly and carefully to his flock of boys. Possessed by nature with a strong innate love of knowledge, he has afforded a striking instance of its acquisition, by turning to good account the peculiar leisure of a shepherd's occupation; and as the simple narrative of his progress refers to many particulars of the former habits of living on the South Downs, I trust the reader will follow with interest the peaceful tenor of his way, as here described in his own words."

John Dudeney was born at Rottingdean on the 21st April, 1782, his father, Henry Dudeney, being shepherd to John Hamshaw. They lived with his grandfather, also named John, "in what is now called Plumpton Cottage, which was then his property."

John was sent to school to an old woman at Plumpton, but as he "only learned to drive ducks into the moat" he was removed from the school in case he followed the ducks. He remarked: "That was all the schooling I ever had!" His mother taught him to read and his father taught him to write a little, also to do addition and subtraction, but that was his father's limit in arithmetic, and John did not learn his multiplication table until he was nearly eighteen.

When eight years old he began to follow the sheep, and sometimes drove the plough. He was fond of reading, and borrowed all the books he could, and when about ten was given a small History of England and a copy of *Robinson Crusoe* by Mr. Dunvan, of Lewes. Afterwards he saved what money he could for books, and when at Lewes Fair purchased a history of France and one of Rome. A book on geography, which his father borrowed, proved particularly interesting to him.

At that time John's mother tended the flock when her husband was away sheep-shearing. Other shepherds' wives occasionally did the same, but later the custom was discontinued, and in his narrative the shepherd wrote : " I have not seen a woman with a flock for several years."

John's master allowed him the keeping of one sheep for himself, the lamb and wool of which brought him 14s. or 15s. a year. This money he saved to buy a watch, which cost four guineas, but it served him for over fifty years. The trapping of wheatears brought him a few extra shillings.

At sixteen years of age he went to West Blatchington as under-shepherd, but only stayed one year. Here, " during a snow " in the winter of 1798-9, the flock was put in a barn-yard, the first instance he knew of sheep being put in a yard except at lambing time. At Midsummer, 1799, he removed to Kingston-by-Lewes, where he acted as under-shepherd for three years. The head shepherd being very old and infirm, he had much to do, but his wages only amounted to £6 a year and part of the small sales of wheatears. In winter he caught moles, which, at twopence each, brought a few shillings to buy more books. His next purchases were Turner's *Introductions to Geography*, *The Arts and Sciences*, and *Astronomy*, also a dictionary and an English grammar. He had little leisure for reading at home, so carried books in his pocket for study at odd times, but his work was never neglected. In 1802 he began his study of practical geometry, and on Newmarket Hill had a hole in the turf, covered by a big stone, in which he stored his books and a slate, so that no opportunity for study was wasted.

His next move was to Rottingdean, as head shepherd to Mr. James Ingram. Westside Farm extended from Rottingdean to Black Rock. The flock, owned by three farmers, needed close attention as there were no fences between the feeding-ground and other land. Fortunately he had an excellent dog, which was a valuable help in keeping the sheep from crossing the boundaries. Along this coast great numbers of wheatears were caught between mid-July and the end of August. The most he ever took was thirteen dozen in a day. They were all sold to a Brighton poulterer at 1s. 6d. a dozen.

At Rottingdean he had greater opportunities for study than ever before. He was helped by the Rev. Dr. Hooker, the vicar, and also by his aunt, with whom he lived. The possession of a Hebrew Bible, grammar, and lexicon gave him great delight.

Mr. Blencowe's account of the shepherd concludes with the following paragraph:

"In 1804 Mr. Dudeney gave up the flock altogether. He came to Lewes, and there opened a school, with, as he modestly says, no other qualification for it than a real love of learning; but, to use his own words, indulging in the hope that it may be justly said of him when he is gone that 'he had been of some little use in his day, and to the generation and place in which he lived.'"

An item of special interest to ornithologists is included in John Dudeney's reminiscences. He remarks that bustards formerly frequented the Downs, but had not been seen for nearly a century. His father saw one about 1750 near to a spot known as Four Lords Dool.

---

*Note.*—In the *Sussex County Magazine* for January, 1930, there is a copy of a paper written by Dudeney. It is an exhaustive account of the capture of wheatears by shepherds, and is accompanied by a portrait of Dudeney and his drawings of a wheatear trap.

---

### STEPHEN BLACKMORE, 1833–1920

In 1920 there passed away, in Steyning workhouse, at the age of eighty-seven, Stephen Blackmore—a former

Sussex shepherd who was born at Falmer. He became famous as a collector of flint implements.

In the novel *Magpie House*, by Andrew Soutar, we read about an old shepherd named Reuben Blunt who collected flint implements. I understand that the account of this character is based on studies of Stephen Blackmore. Mr. Arthur Beckett knew the shepherd, and the following note is copied, with his permission, from *The Spirit of the Downs*:

" Stephen Blackmore, an old shepherd friend of mine (now retired from active life) has made a valuable collection of Neolithic implements of the neighbourhood of East Dean and Beachy Head, which were found by him on the hills and in the valleys while tending sheep during a period extending over many years. Blackmore's collection of Neolithic implements is considered to be one of the finest in private hands in this country, including, as it does, several beautiful specimens, both chipped and ground. I remember several years ago incurring the old man's wrath by reason of a newspaper article which I wrote concerning the collection, the result of which was, said the owner, that he was 'worrited to death by a gen'leman from one o' they Lunnon museums.' Blackmore, although always pleased to show his collection to anyone who expressed the wish, was always jealous of it; and I never knew him inclined to part with any of the best specimens, even when he was badly in need of money."

When corresponding with Mr. G. Hemming, of Headcorn, I learned that he and his wife had been enthusiastic ramblers on the Sussex Downs years ago and that they had known Stephen Blackmore. Mrs. Hemming had some notes about him, which she wrote about 1906, among her records, also a photograph of him taken by

Mr. Hemming in 1903. These they very kindly offered for use in this book and I gladly took advantage of the opportunity to add such an intimate description of this famous old shepherd and his wife.

SOME NOTES ON STEPHEN BLACKMORE, SHEPHERD AND FLINT-FINDER : BY MRS. G. HEMMING

We had often heard of old Stephen Blackmore, the one-armed shepherd of East Dean, and we had seen the collection of flints—some good, many of them indifferent —which he had given to the Museum in Lewes Castle, so we went one day to East Dean to find him.

Stephen's cottage, Frost Hill, was a good square cottage, set off the road upon the Downs that slope towards Beachy Head. His wife opened the door. She was a handsome old lady, with bright, wild dark eyes and pretty pink cheeks, and really magnificent wavy white hair. She wore then, as always, a black netted cap, and a cross-over of red and black plaid in large checks, and a plain dark skirt. This almost peasant costume accentuated her picturesqueness. She received us without surprise, rather with an implied manner that it was indeed natural that we should wish to pay homage at such a shrine. Stephen was out, but she showed us the great man's home, his books, and a rough deal cabinet with glass doors, within which were a good many stones. But it was locked ! " Oh, yes, he always keeps it locked, he do ! " she said, and laughed shrilly, with a kind of admiration for Stephen's suspicious care. The walls of the kitchen were hung with several photographs of Stephen—Stephen in his long shepherd's coat, Stephen with his dog, and an admirable photograph of Stephen and herself standing by the garden wall, he with his crook and rough clothes and wearing a curious tall square hat, she in a sunbonnet, and the sheep-dog between them. We admired it. " Oh, yes, but we are *generally* taken by

Photo by: Dr. Habberton Lulham

"OFF TO THE HILLS"

*Photo by Dr. Habberton Lalham*

# JIM FOWLER

the kitchen door; that's where they generally photograph *us*," she said.

Just as we were going Stephen and his dog, "Boxer," came in. "Boxer" was a black and white old English sheep-dog. Dog after dog, all through the long course of Stephen's shepherding, all his dogs had been "Boxers." They marked kind of epochs. "That was in the days of 'Boxer's' father (or of his grandfather)," Stephen would say.

Stephen Blackmore was a fine-looking man, though rather small. He had a broad, intelligent forehead, and a fine head of wavy snow-white hair, a white beard, bushy white eyebrows, and little deep-set, cunning blue eyes. He unlocked the cabinet and showed us the implements. Then, as always, whatever you wanted to buy was just the best, the rarest, and consequently the dearest —or someone else would be after it, too, to enhance its value. On the other hand, he was not without a certain native dignity—the dignity of a man who for so many years had lived face to face with Nature, alone on the Downs. He was a clever shepherd, kind to his sheep and to his dog. His wife was devoted to him, and I think he had been a good father. He had read a good deal, though the Bible was his one book, and from it he acquired at times a somewhat stately diction. When I knew him better and he often talked about it I could see that he was poetical, too, and that he attached a certain mystic significance to his own office of being a shepherd. Nature he knew and loved in all her moods.

Notoriety in a little place—the big storm in a little teacup—had helped to deteriorate him. He had had some distinguished visitors—Sir John Evans, Charles Kingsley, Lord Avebury, and Benjamin Harrison, of Ightam.

Sometimes he came flint hunting with us, but it is an arduous occupation, and one best done alone. It demands great concentration and is very tiring. You walk along, furrow by furrow, glancing at every stone, and you can only search with comfort when the light is behind you, and when the rains have partially washed the stones.

I bought from Stephen two large rough celts (battle-axes, he called them), and I remember now the superstitious reverence with which he told me that he had found them just below the Old Eastbourne Lighthouse lying almost side by side, only a few yards apart, made and owned, as he believed it, by the same man. "Understand," said he, "he was a *left-handed man*." This was a favourite formula. He would take up a stone and hold it in his left, his only hand, until he got it into a comfortable position, and then point out that its maker must have been a left-handed man. There was simplicity in this because Stephen had no right hand with which to test any implement. He had lost his right arm when he was seventeen in an accident with a threshing machine.

He said that when hunting he often saw stones and he was afraid to pick them up or to "hack them out with his heel" for fear of disappointment. A magnificent underside and bulb of percussion often, on the upper side, results only in an untrimmed flake struck off a nodule. The implements we found were either of the Cave or early Neolithic period. (Stephen made curious sketches of his best finds, every chip marked blackly in, till they were more like maps of stones than sketches.) Smuggling once went on at Cuckmere, and Stephen told of kegs of brandy run in there in his grandfather's time, and of how his grandmother had a dress of silk brought in in the same way. "Grand days, those!" he sighed.

'Tis true whatever stones I found Stephen would say: "Ah, I have found better than that—and blue 'uns and black 'uns!" He laid great stress on blue and black specimens which, as all flint-hunters know, are more chalcedonic than the white ones.

He told me how his mother had taken a dislike to him when he lost his arm. He thought it was because it took from his value as a bread-winner, and he spoke as if this were a very natural feeling. But his father, he said, was a very just man, who brought him up in the fear of God. He said how once, when a boy, occasion having offered to do some little service for a gentleman (I think it was to hold his horse), he had begged, and money had been given to him. "But my father, if he had known, he would have thrashed me!"

He then went on to tell me how his wife was his first cousin, and what a beautiful woman she had been when she was young, which I well believe, and how, having lost his arm, he had "no thought to wed," but that she was then earning good wages in service at Seaford, and she knew that his mother was unkind to him at home. So one Sunday afternoon they had gone for a walk together, he having no such thoughts in his mind. Towards evening they had neared his father's house and the sun was setting, and she turned to him suddenly and said: "Stephen, shall us be wed?"—and she blushed a sudden bright beautiful colour all over neck and brow. Well, they were married, and he became shepherd, and when the children came he was very tender of them too. They were other little lambs, even more helpless, that needed his care. The simple events of life—all natural causes, paternity, maternity—all these had deep significance for Stephen.

One day we were going to Lewes and we happed upon him near Seaford station, and he at once expressed his determination to come with us. In Lewes we encountered a flock of sheep, and I asked him to guess their number. Stephen stalked alongside of them in the street, counting and considering. People turned to look at the noticeable white-haired old man. He guessed the number to be 120, and then asked the shepherd. The right number was 122.

We used sometimes to have Stephen and his wife to tea with us in our lodgings, when we took care to provide good entertainment. They came, a sober decent old couple, the old lady, on these occasions, forsaking her red plaid for black silk. Stephen said a solemn grace in a loud voice, and Mrs. Blackmore always ate dry bread and then honey in a teaspoon, which seemed to me a very sensible arrangement. Great was then their talk of how Stephen had had a great admiration for Stanley, the explorer, and a desire to read his books. He had named his grandson after him, and the Geological Society, somehow hearing of this, had sent him Stanley's works. We were told how one day, long ago, he had fallen asleep out-of-doors at Seaford. When he awoke a man stood over him, and the man put a book into Stephen's hand and departed without a word. The man was Charles Kingsley, and the book was *The Water Babies.*

Sometimes Stephen's tales were rather vague and very complicated. Such was the great and heroic epic of how, at much risk and with infinite bravery, he had driven some of his sheep through Falmer tunnel, thereby saving their lives from an on-coming train, but endangering his own.

I remember very well the last time I ever saw " de old lady," as Stephen used to call his wife. He always used the Sussex " de " and " dat " for " the " and " that." Stephen was not very well—he had been bitten in the leg by a dog. We asked him " what kind of a dog ? " He said : " Understand it was de dog of Urry, and he wur a big black one, but I don't know what species." Urry was the Seaford coalman, and I thought that " the dog of Urry " had a biblical sound. Stephen rubbed Friar's

Balsam and honey and salt into the bite, and it did it good, though he said it made him "holler."

Soon after this they moved into the Seaford almshouses, and Mrs. Blackmore only survived the moving by a fortnight. Stephen wrote me the news of her death. He said: "She was serviceable to the last of her life and died in Pease. I am lonely now. Bess so many years has been a good wife, my dear friend. It seems she did not suffer." A stately photograph still exists of Elizabeth Blackmore—a Rembrandtesque thing, in profile, with a side-light on her clear-cut features and on her beautiful wavy white hair. She was the better of the two, the wittier, the more self-respecting. With her death Stephen became careless of himself.

In his book, *Talks with Shepherds*, Mr. Walter Johnson has given us an entertaining chapter describing his visit to Blackmore while the shepherd was living in retirement at an almshouse at Seaford. Mr. Johnson states that it was then too late (1912) to interview him with a view to obtaining detailed information concerning his life among the sheep, which would have been of interest, but every "flint" enthusiast who reads the chapter must feel indebted to the author for his sympathetic description of the old shepherd and his treasured stones, and must turn the last page with a feeling of regret that he did not share Mr. Johnson's experience.

## SOME TYPICAL SHEPHERDS

ALTHOUGH a book could be filled with portraits and biographies of shepherds the accounts of the few recorded here must represent the whole number. These have been specially selected to show that actual interviews have resulted in the gathering of facts relating to old days and ways and valuable notes on various subjects. My pile of note-books proves how numberless visits to shepherds resulted in the collection of a store of information, without which it would have been impossible to compile such a book as this or to obtain a true and intimate knowledge of their lives.

### NELSON COPPARD[1]

Nelson Coppard was born at Poynings in 1863. His father was shepherd on Dyke Hill for eighteen years. He started work very early as shepherd boy at Horton, near Beeding. Then he became teg boy to Eli Page, of Patcham, and later he served as under-shepherd at Saddlescombe. Since then he has been shepherd at Trueleigh, Iford, America (between Firle and Newhaven), Balmer near Falmer, and Mary Farm, Falmer. He is now at Pangdean Farm by Clayton Mills.

To write a full account of Mr. Coppard as I know him would be a long story. He was the first shepherd I ever met. From him I had my first instruction on sheep-bells, crooks, and the details of a shepherd's life. To the lucky natives of Sussex a meeting with a shepherd is

[1] See frontispiece.

just an ordinary incident in a Downland ramble, but to a Londoner, blessed with an artistic temperament, that first sudden entry into a little valley full of sheep with their ancient bells chiming, the meeting with a jovial shepherd with his glittering crook, the chat with him, and the return journey, when I carried home wild flowers and two large canister bells, was overwhelming. I felt that I had stepped into a new world.

My anxiety to learn amused the shepherd. It was a fresh experience for him to find anybody so eager for the information he could impart. Though I have since found many shepherds and gathered a store of memories, I do not forget that our first meeting was the start of a long series of rambles which have at last ended in the making of this record.

There is always something of interest or something quaint to note down after a visit to Nelson. To-day, as I stood on the hill by Pyecombe Church, I could see his fold at the edge of Pangdean Farm. I was not expecting to hear much music from sheep-bells, knowing that it is his custom to remove most of them and keep them in his hut at this time of year; I was therefore startled by the deafening burst of sound which greeted me as I approached the fold. The din did not stop until I actually passed the first barrier of wattles and furze branches. Behind these I found the shepherd and his son-in-law, Ted Nutley, holding the bells and laughing heartily at their success in "ringing me in." "I was just taking the bells into the hut," explained Nelson, "when Nutley saw you coming along. I know you like to hear the bells when you come, so we rung 'em for ye!"

After dinner we inspected the flock. The shepherd pointed out a dead lamb. It was well grown, but had collapsed and died suddenly, as is sometimes the case. We fetched the ewes from another fold. The flock spread out, as mothers and children, making a babel of cries in various keys, sorted themselves and were gradually united. One ewe, wandering about and calling plaintively for her baby, at last found the body of the lamb. Nelson approached, crook in hand; caught the ewe and examined her. "Thought so!" he exclaimed; "she be full of milk!" and he led her into the fold and secured her in a pen. Then he sharpened his knife, fetched the dead lamb, cut through its skin round the joints of the forelegs and slit down the chest, and in a few minutes off came its woolly jacket, quite clean and inside out. This was at once turned, fitted with strings and hung on a stick ready for use. A lamb that was not getting milk owing to the temporary sickness of its mother was caught and dressed in the dead lamb's skin. He was quite big enough for it—it fitted him as closely as a suit of combinations when it was tied on. The lamb's movements provoked a smile, and Nelson said: "He be like we when *we* gets a new suit—it don't feel jus' right at first!"

The ears on the skin gave the baby a quaint appearance; at first sight one might have thought that a lamb with four ears was on show. Now began the troublesome task of persuading the baby to feed from its foster-mother. After many patient efforts the shepherd succeeded, and although the ewe sniffed suspiciously at the lamb at first the two had accepted each other before we left them.

Mr. Coppard's flocks have varied greatly in number on various farms, but he states that in a general way the flocks kept now are much smaller than in past days. Many other changes have taken place. He has no use now for the big dipping hook which he used at the sheep-wash, as this part of the shepherds' work has died out in most districts.

I questioned him about sheep marking. Ordinary

marking on the wool with a stick dipped in colour has been his usual practice, but he has had many sheep earmarked with holes and snicks in the ears, also some few pedigree sheep which had " ear-rings "—small brass or other metal tickets fastened to the ear by a ring. Tattooed marks inside the ear stamped with a special punch are now found in Southdown sheep from registered flocks. A ewe was caught for inspection. The flock number, " 550," was stamped inside, and there was also a round hole punched through near the tip and a triangular snick taken out of the edge. Punched marks are often used as a record of age, and are a more reliable guide than the animals' teeth.

I was collecting notes about shepherds' clothes and Mr. Coppard stated that good corduroy suits and gaiters, with a hard felt " bowler " hat had been his usual dress, but his father wore a smock, " a blue one," he said, " not like the slaty-colour one I got for you, but blue— what you might call a *butcher blue*. He always wore that over his corduroys, and in bad weather an overcoat on top o' that! I only wish I had one o' those overcoats," he remarked, " but you couldn' get such a thing nowadays. They were thick and rough and fleecy. I remember my father wore a *white* one, though there were all sorts about. In my young days a shepherd could sometimes get hold of an old cavalry cloak. They were fine things to keep ye dry!"

Nelson is noted among other shepherds for his fondness for sheep-bells and good dogs. He says there used to be far more dogs of the rough-haired type in his young days, and fewer collies than at present. A stranger once said to him: " Your dog obeys you well, shepherd— you must have payed him pretty much to get him to obey you like he does!" Nelson could hardly believe that he had heard aright. At last he said: " If I ' payed ' *you*, as you calls it, would you do any work for me afterwards?" "No, I wouldn't," said the stranger, "I guess I'd keep out of your way." "Very well, then," exclaimed Nelson, "'tis the same with a dog—you got to teach by *talking* to him, *not* by *paying* him. You'll *never* teach a dumb animal to like you by *paying* him!"

The shepherd has a keen sense of humour, and a very dry way, as those who chat to him soon discover. His quaint answers and remarks have already provided me with material for many paragraphs. He told me of his interview with "an old grey-whiskered gentleman in riding kit" who had just returned from a hunt. "Dear me, shepherd," he said, "my feet ache and my legs ache so much I don't know how to walk." "Well, I suppose you've bin on 'em a good time, haven't ye?" asked Nelson. "No," said the hunter, "it isn't that, for I've been riding all day!" Whereupon Nelson remarked, in his usual dry way, "You don't get my meaning—I mean you've *had 'em* a good long time, surely!"—and then the old gentleman saw the joke.

Other little tales and comments passed the time away. Nelson had saved some old ox shoes he had found and told me that black runts, used for ploughing and other work, were once bought and sold at Steyning. Then the mention of Michael Blann's name recalled the fact that Mr. Blann once cut out a sundial in the turf for him to use. He was shepherd boy in those days. He stayed out all day and was provided with his lunch. This was generally the top of a loaf. Sometimes it was pulled open on the soft side and some butter put in it, but if there was no butter he had a piece of fat bacon out of the brine crock. He recalled a certain day when he sat on the brow of a high hill to have his lunch with a companion. The loaf-top slipped from his hand, and rolled and bumped and danced all down the slope "like a cannon-ball." They both laughed to see it go. It was too far to fetch it, and Nelson lost his lunch, but the loss was forgotten in amusement at the incident, and to-day the thought of that rolling loaf-top still brings a smile to his face.

It is refreshing to meet with anybody so outspoken as this shepherd. " I think it be the best way," he once remarked to me. " I says what I thinks, an' I talks in front o' people as I talks behind their backs ! If what you *thinks* be right then, what you *says* will be right too ! "

I could still write many pages about Nelson Coppard, but those who wish can find him on the hills and prove for themselves that he can be a very entertaining companion.[1]

## JACK COX

It was a fortunate day for me when I tramped over the hills from Washington to Lee Farm and found Jack Cox, the shepherd. Such courtesy ! Such readiness to listen to my request for information ! Such willingness to assist !

On the green bank opposite his house I explained my errand, watched all the while by Jim; a beautiful white sheep-dog. Our conversation soon drifted to details of shepherd-craft. Mr. Cox has a Pyecombe crook, light in weight, and about thirty years old, so this must have been made by Mr. Mitchell. It is rather a poor specimen now, but it is still the shepherd's favourite. His son had a nice new crook of local make, but Mr. Cox does not covet it. He tried it for the first time in front of the farmer (a practical man) and missed a catch, much to the farmer's surprise. He explained about the new crook, and returned to his old " Pyecombe." He said : " Directly you have tried a crook you know, somehow, if it will do for you. Now, this old hook will hold any sheep for me, and it has never failed ! "

[1] While this book was being printed Nelson Coppard retired from work.

The shepherd used to wear a smock, and told me a fresh item of interest in connection with shepherds' dress. He has known shepherds, when beginning work, such as fold pitching, to change from smock and hard hat into a rough sacking slop and a red cap ("well, a little cap, anyway, most times a red one"). "A hard hat was in the way when carrying hurdles, which would sometimes touch the hat and tilt it over your eyes."

I was anxious to see the shepherd's old canister bells, for, as I told him, I had listened to them on a former visit to Harrow Hill when I was hunting for flint implements. My joy in the sudden discovery of a beautiful flint axe while the songs of the bells were borne to me on the breeze made that ramble a memorable one. To-day the bells were silent; they had been removed for shearing time, but the shepherd took me to the lambing yard to see them. In the corner was a little room, with hearth and chimney. His arm-chair was there—a low-backed one. "This is how I sit before the fire at lambing time," he said. "My father taught me to do it," and as he spoke he demonstrated for my benefit. "If I doze," he said, "my head wags and drops, and I start up and know 'tis time to move again, or I might sleep too long. My father said that was the way. 'Sit orkard,' he used to say, 'sit orkard an' you won't sleep too long,' and so I always do it!"

The precious bells were hanging in the room, and while I inspected them he told me that in war time he had a flock of nine hundred to look after. His wife was his only assistant, so she donned shepherd's clothes, and between them they did all that was required.

The shepherd enjoys his life among the hills. "I wouldn't live in the town," he said. "If you want a pound of potatoes you go to a shop and buy them; if you want a few sticks of wood to light a fire you go to a shop and buy them! No, the wages may be less in the country, but you save in many small ways, and you live in the finest air there is!"

Before I left, he allowed me to select a bell for my collection, and I chose an old well-worn canister with a wooden yoke. "These bells," he said, "came from a shepherd named Michael Blann, years ago. *He* was one of the old shepherds, and ought to be included in your book. If he is still alive he must be old; he was living at Patching when I last heard of him."

I packed the precious bell in my satchel—a souvenir of a very pleasant visit to Lee Farm—and wandered home over the hills.

At a later date I met the shepherd again as he was returning to the farm with his flock. The dog Jim was with him. "Don't touch him," said Mr. Cox; "he is rather sore about the head." They had found a badger, abroad in daylight, a few days before, and when it ran into a little hurdle pen in the corner of the field and tried to hide in a hole in the bank Jim attacked it. He received a nasty bite, but the badger was killed. Mr. Cox remarked that it showed he must be a strong dog and very plucky to have tackled a badger so fearlessly.

As we stood listening to the songs of the canister bells on the sheep he talked about the scarcity of shepherd boys. He said that at present there are plenty of shepherds, but so few boys training for the work. The mere minding of sheep for a few hours is simple enough, but there is so much to learn before one can be called a shepherd. He mentioned a man who thought the shepherd's life an ideal one, and willingly tried it for a day. He accompanied Mr. Cox early in the morning. He found it difficult to pick up three hurdles on a pole, to carry them and put them down correctly. "They went round on the pole like windmill sweeps," said the shepherd. His next experience—that of pitching a fold—was equally disappointing. The iron bar seemed to make so many holes in the ground, instead of only one big enough for the stake. "That was only *two* things out of the day's work, as I told him," said Mr. Cox. "All that I told him to do *I* learned forty years ago, and every year since I have learned something fresh about sheep that I didn't know before! That is why a man of my age could not start as a shepherd now—he would always be forty years behind!"

The day was cold and dull, but a very short and very precious sunny interval, when we met, enabled me to procure a photograph of the shepherd and his beautiful dog.

## Michael Blann

I asked a little girl in a Patching lane if she knew where Mr. Blann lived. She answered: "Yes, sir, he lives in the first cottage on that side." Then she added, very seriously: "He's got a long beard, right down to here," and she touched her little knees. Thus when I arrived at the cottage and saw a man just coming to the door from the meadow at the side I knew that I had found the shepherd I sought, although the length of his beard was less than I expected from the child's description.

We were soon chatting, and I learned that Michael Blann comes from a Sussex family. His father was born at Sompting, and Michael was born at Beeding in 1843. Although his family were not shepherds, he was put to the work when nine years old, and stayed at it. His wages were 3s. 6d. a week, although at that date some boys received only 2s. 6d. A shepherd's wage in his young days was 12s. or 13s. a week—"not much when you come to think of it," he said. True, he had his house as well, sometimes, but even then to bring up a family on such a wage wanted some doing, and there was not much left for the shepherd!

We spoke of Findon Fair. "It is only a sheep sale

now," said Mr. Blann. "I remember the first time I went to Findon Fair—seventy-seven years ago, when I was only ten years old. I had to mind the flock up at the end of the field while shepherd went to find the pens he was to use. Near to me was a thing like a round table with hooks all round it. It was set near to a big fire. A pig was cut up and the joints were hung on the hooks. The big turnspit took the joints round and round, and when they were cooked folks bought roast pork for their dinner."

While speaking of clothes worn by shepherds I told him of Mr. Cox's reference to caps worn when pitching, and he confirmed this, as he wore one for the same purpose. Referring to wattles hitting a shepherd's hat, he said: "Some shepherds had dog's-hair hats—you don't see them now! They were something like a billy-cock, but very thick and very strong. They were heavy to wear when working or in the sun, and so a cap was carried in the pocket." One short man he knew who had occasion to reach something high up stood on his hat to do it!

The shepherd wore a round frock for many years, and longer than some who felt "old-fashioned" in one. He told me of the large, heavy overcoats. They were fleecy outside, and very thick, with a big cape. He was once fortunate enough to own a white one. When it was at last worse for wear he turned it very carefully and sewed it together again with twine to make it last as long as possible. His wife made his smocks for him. The last one was made to his own idea to open all down the front. "I somehow got tired of pulling it off over my head," he said, "although everybody knows that is the way to get out of a smock."

Outside the cottage lay the remains of a big cask. It must have been old and dry, for when a passing waggon touched it it collapsed. "It all fell to bits in once!"

said Mr. Blann. (The thought of it always amused him.) He moved the pieces with his stick, and revealed several short bits of curved branches which he had cut for making sheep-bell yokes. He showed me how some could be split to make two yokes instead of one. (How deeply must the charm of bells bore into a shepherd's heart if it causes a man of eighty-seven to cut yokes which he will never use!) "I was very fond of my bells," he said, "and very particular to keep my tackle in good order. I had one little canister which I once heard from two miles away. I was always fond of it after that. I cut out all my own wooden crooks (bell yokes) and bone lockyers, and took great pride in them. Now Jack Cox has them all; he has had them a good many years, so he knows they were good bells and tackle."

In reply to my enquiry, Mr. Blann said he had never seen bells for sale at Lewes Fair. "I reckon that must have been a good time ago," he remarked.

I also asked about his crook, but learned that he had parted with it long ago to "a man who took it away to London."

According to the shepherd's opinion, modern "progress" has not improved us. His comment was, "People are not so content nowadays, even with all they've got! They're always rooshing about, and yet they have time to pick one another to pieces! They don't try to help one another, or put one another together a bit!"

Mr. Blann loves music. At one time he could play several instruments. He was well known as a singer, and often sang in company with a friend. "I enjoyed that," he said, "for we got on very well together." He would sing alone if asked, and was often called upon for a song at fair "sing-songs," shearing parties and local entertainments. He has a book in which he wrote the words of all his favourite songs. It was started in 1867

*Photos by Dr. Habberton Lulham*

"THE CHANGELING"

**THE SHEPHERD'S UMBRELLA**
Two studies of George Humphrey of Steyning

*Photos by the Author*

and is a precious possession. It was once borrowed by a collector of old songs, who would not return it, but another enthusiast turned up, and hearing that the first man had kept the book for years, went after it, and at last the shepherd had his treasured book again.

Mr. Blann also has his favourite flute, but finds it less easy to play than formerly. He was surprised at my delight when he produced another treasure—a tin whistle which he always carried in his pocket, so that he could play to himself on the hills while minding a flock. It was also useful at times for pitching on the correct note quickly when starting a song. I sat by him while he sang a verse of four of his favourites to me and played the tunes slowly on the whistle pipe for my benefit. I listened to " Sheep Shearing," " The Harvest Home," " A Drop of Good Beer," and " Rock the Cradle, John ! " and thus I was linked for the first time with the old sheep-shearing suppers of years ago when the gang called on Michael for a song.

I had read of shepherds using reed pipes and whistle pipes, and had found pictures portraying such scenes, but it was delightful to one engaged on a Sussex shepherds' book to prove an actual instance in the county.

Mr. Blann also used " Jew's harps," and carried them with him, but the whistle pipe was his favourite.

A reference to horn lanterns caused the shepherd to point to a box near the broken cask. " There is one in there," he said. He got it out and offered it to me. It was very old and rusted, but the horn windows were still in good condition, and I accepted it gladly. " It oughtn't to have been left out in the wet," he remarked, " but I offered it to somebody and he didn't trouble to come to take it, and there it has been waiting for him ! " After wrapping up the lantern for me he said : " I always used a horn lantern except once. That was when I had an oil lamp for lambing time, about twenty-five years ago. One night, in a turr'ble wind and a snowstorm, I had to move a lamb. With the lamb and the lamp held in front of me I walked backwards in the snow, for I could not face the wind. I didn't know the snow had covered a ewe right in, and back I went over her. The lamp broke, the oil caught fire, and I had to move pretty quickly to beat it out. It *was* a mess! After that I never would use an oil lamp again, so I sent to Brighton for this one. He's been a good lantern! 'Tis a pity he's rusted so!"

But the lantern is now in order again. A careful repair to the base and a thorough cleaning worked wonders, and the old specimen is once more a treasured possession and a link with Michael Blann.

During the three years I knew Michael I went to see him several times. A chat with a visitor acted as a tonic, and head-pains and other uncomfortable ailments were forgotten for a time. It was a pleasure to tell me items of information which he thought might interest me. He had been a clever workman in many ways, and had made all kinds of things for his own use. His tools and all sorts of oddments which " might prove useful some day " were wrapped neatly in little parcels, and his only trouble was that they were hidden in so many boxes. This objection to throwing away things that may be useful at a later date is a common failing in many of us. In the case of a poor shepherd, obliged to do many jobs himself to save expense, it is a natural trait, and Michael's habit of storing oddments lasted all his life. When he passed away, at the age of ninety, his wife moved from the cottage and Michael's possessions were at last unpacked from the boxes in which they were stored. His sheep-shears were found in a flat leather protector, marked " M. B.", in a parcel. They were clean and sharp, and oiled ready for instant use, although he had been too old to use them for many years. Tools had been kept in order, and endless little packages revealed heaps of oddments, even to odd lots of nails and screws wrapped in papers. It was a surprising collection, but I understood the reason for it. One day, as Michael had looked for the vice and saw with which he cut out yokes and lockyers for sheep-bells, he had told me why he had been forced to do all this careful packing. He once owned a big chest, which held all the treasured bits, but a lady who called (and who, I think, must have found a bargain) wished to buy the chest and to take it away at once. The idea of turning out the contents and having them in a heap distressed Michael, but as the lady said that if he did it she would give him ten pounds he accepted the offer. " I didn't want to do it," he said to me, " but I thought to myself, ' Well, you'd best do it, for you only gave a pound for the chest, and you will have nine pound profit.' I wanted the money, so out came all the things, and so I've been in this turrible muddle ever since,—but there 'tis,—*throw anything away, and sure enough the day comes when you wish you had it back!*"

## WALTER WOOLER

At the top of the steep path which starts at the farm buildings opposite Pyecombe post office, I found Mr. Walter Wooler, one of the oldest shepherds working in East Sussex.

I was delighted to discover that I had arrived in time to see him mark his sheep and lambs ready for Lewes sheep sale.

A number of small hurdle pens next to the fold contained the different lots of animals, and leading from the largest one was a long pointed pen with a movable hurdle at the wide end for a door.

I entered the fold to watch the shepherd at his task. Near the long pen a little hollow held his fire. A brick on either side supported the iron bars on which stood a pot of hot pitch. Deftly the shepherd dipped the marking iron into the pitch, shook off the drips, leaned over the hurdles and marked the wool of one of the lambs packed in the narrow pen. A dozen times he did this, then, after resting the marking iron on the pot, he lifted the heavy pitching iron from its place at the point of the pen, thereby releasing a hurdle to allow the lambs to escape. Out they ran, all clearly marked with an M in a circle (the farmer's initial) and joined the others in the fold.

Again he started methodically. He replaced the hurdle and the iron; he entered the large pen, pushed the hurdle back after him and opened the door of the triangular pen. Next he unshackled the hurdle door of a small pen and released the inmates, drove some of them into the triangle, closed the door and shackled it, came out into the fold by his own door, closed it and shackled it. Then he blew his fire up, fed it with a handful of wood (bits of a worn-out hurdle), and took a drink of cocoa from a bottle. "Time ago I had a mate at these times," he said, "to hold the sheep and mend the fire and so on, but though it takes longer alone, I do it as well by packing them in the pen tightly so they can't run about." Once more the marking iron was dipped, shaken, and used time after time and replaced over the pot. Once more the pitching iron was removed and the same tedious process repeated with clockwork regularity. In some cases a further marking with a dot of red paint was also necessary. This was done with a stick dipped in the paint can. One could not help noting the precision with which every little movement was accomplished— a striking example of life-long, methodical habit. At last the work was finished. We drove the flock to their feeding ground, and after an interval for dinner I doddled along with the shepherd to the fold.

Mr. Wooler was born at Alfriston in 1856, and was

brought to Pyecombe when only three months old. His father was shepherd to Mr. Blaker of Pyecombe for many years. Walter's natural aptitude for the care of sheep and his thorough training are proved by the fact that at sixteen years of age he had charge of a flock of five hundred ewes belonging to Mr. Blaker and lambed them down by himself. Fifty-eight times since then has lambing time come and gone, and still he carries on with the same eager delight. He left Pyecombe once and lived at Alfriston, and married, but returned to Pyecombe and stayed there, so, as he remarked, he "knows the place very well."

A "round frock" and white corduroys was once his usual dress. With a smock and big umbrella he was not afraid of a wet day.

In course of conversation I asked if he had ever used a cave or a "shepherd's bush," and found that he had used a hole in a bank "like the beginning of a cave" for resting in at times. Some furze branches put round the outside improved it. He had also taken a bill-hook out with him sometimes to cut away a convenient bush so that he could "back" into it and put his big umbrella over him. These shelters were only used when they commanded a view of the feeding-ground. He had not known this to be done by shepherds as a usual practice, but did it for his own convenience.

Mr. Wooler's crook was made for him by Mr. Charles Mitchell at Pyecombe forge more than fifty years ago. It split and was repaired recently. He once owned a brass crook, which broke, as most of them did. He was able to confirm the fact that these crooks were made at a Brighton railway workshop, for he knew the man who made them.

I found that the shepherd could speak with authority on the subject of sheep diseases, and agrees that every shepherd should have the power to kill or to recommend the killing of any sheep to save suffering. His father cured mild cases of "foot and mouth disease" with blue vitriol and boiled vinegar. Further conversation on the care of sheep and his day's work brought us back to the subject of sheep-marking. All the usual marks were known to him, and I was pleased to find that he remembered the use of a farthing as a marker, and spoke of sheep having a "farthing mark" in the ear. (This is referred to in a separate note on markings.) He promised to give me an old marking iron with the letter S (the initial of Mr. Scrace, the farmer there for many years). This proved to be a nice old tool, still bearing a coating of pitch on parts of its surface.

It was a wonderful thing to have gathered information on so many points by a casual chat with Walter Wooler. I look back on my visit with delight. I remember his quiet courtesy and his kindly interest in my desire to record precious little details. The picture that remains with me is that of the black pitch pot on the little fire, and the dear old shepherd by the long hurdle pen with the marking iron in his hand.

*Note.*—A portrait of Walter Wooler appears with the notes on shepherds' clothes.

### George Humphrey

George Humphrey was a well-known figure on the Sompting hills. I have often passed a few minutes with him, and he has supplied me with interesting information on several occasions. To-day he had time for a chat—a rather unusual thing for him, for although, like most old shepherds, he deplores the passing of ways and customs of past years, his opinions do not affect his daily work, and he is a busy man.

Mr. Humphrey was born at Canada, near Withdean, in 1864. His father was brought to Sussex as a boy when the grandfather was shepherd to the Duke of Richmond at Boxgrove. He was thus used to the details of the craft from his earliest years and his training was strict.

"I often think of that time!" he said to me to-day. 'In those days everything was done neatly and carefully; there was pride and delight in every job; but now there's no time for pride and delight in anything! The way things are done now is *disgraceful*, but nobody cares, so things don't alter!"

The shepherd stood thinking for a minute. His thoughts were far away from the present day at that moment. "Now, take such a thing as herbs," he said; "most people know nothing about herbs and their virtues. It was different when I was a boy! My mother used to make her own ointment and stuff. Mallow, 'flannel-leaf' and two other plants were used to make ointment. Father and mother went out together collecting herbs when the plants were in their prime and full of virtue.

"Once I was doctoring sheep for foot-rot in a field by the roadside, and an old gipsy woman—a little, shrivelled-up old girl she was—looked over at me. 'You'll never do any good with 'em,' she called out. 'I'll bring you something to-morrow for that.' And so she did," said the shepherd. "I used the stuff she brought and it cured the sheep quicker than anything I've ever known. I offered her all I could afford for the secret of it, but she wouldn't tell it though I offered her a pound! She sold the stuff at half a crown a pot. After that I tried to see what herbs she picked, but her basket had a lid, and if anyone came near her, down went the lid and you couldn't see anything!

"Do you know that a sore place, a bad hand, or anything can be cured by 'Jack in the hedge'?" asked Mr. Humphrey. "First you put on leaves to draw the wound, fresh every time, of course; then more leaves turned the other way up to heal it.

"When I was a boy carters used to pick the flowers and shoots of elderberry and make a lotion with them and take some and a pad of rag to the fields when flies were about. Any spot on a horse that attracted flies was dabbed with the lotion and that soon sent off the flies! They thought of the comfort of their horses in those days!

"The carters used to sing as they drove," remarked the shepherd, "and the horses liked it. Sheep be fond of music too. I've heard shepherd boys play whistle pipes sometimes, and the sheep listened and liked the sound." I told him about Michael Blann, his whistle pipe and song-book. "I never played a whistle pipe," he said, "only a jew's harp, but I liked the songs we used to hear! Real songs they were, and lots of them had lines in them to remember. Now we hear all sorts of rubbish, and there isn't any music in the lot!"

I then asked Mr. Humphrey whether he had ever used a cave, or shepherd's bush. "Yes," he said, "I had one place on these hills which I made with a pick and shovel in a rabbit bury. I could sit in it and watch the sheep. I once had another place near Selsey, in a thorn bush. I cut some of the bush away and put dry fern and straw and stuff inside, and some sacks. It was a handy place on wet days. I could get in it and look out at the flock. It would have taken three days' rain to wet it through."

At the mention of a smock as a protection in bad weather he told me some interesting facts about the shepherds' dress in his boyhood. "When I was a boy," he said, "I had three brothers. Father and us four boys made five to dress, and we all wore corduroy—buff colour—and corduroy gaiters too. We all wore smock frocks over that—blue ones. My mother made all the clothes (and looked a long time at a shilling before spending it), but the stuff was good then! We couldn't afford leather gaiters ; she made us cord gaiters to match the suits and lined them with canvas, and they kept out as much wet as the leather gaiters I buy now do ! Every year, after harvest, mother went off to the shops and bought a big roll of corduroy, and canvas, buttons, thread, and things, and we all had a suit in turn. She made our smocks, too, all tuckered up proper, with big turn-down collars, and pockets that 'd take a rabbit easily without showing it if you walked upright. Overcoats ? Well, yes, we did have one of a sort, but anything had to do. We had good suits and smocks, and there wasn't much money left for overcoats."

A chat on sheep-marks ended this interesting interview, and Mr. Humphrey gave me some valuable information relating to marking of sheep with a " farthing " mark. This is given in detail in the pages devoted to the subject.

## CHARLES TRIGWELL

At Findon Fair I met Jesse Moulding of Goring, the last of several generations of Sussex shepherds. He sat on a wattle by his sheep, for the sale had commenced. " Do you know Charlie Trigwell is here ? " he asked, and pointed to where this old shepherd rested while he surveyed the scene. I took the opportunity to act as messenger, and in a few minutes Mr. Trigwell came back with me for a chat. He used to be a well-known figure at the fairs until ill-health put an end to his work, and this time he was only present as a visitor. I told him about my shepherds' book, and before I left him arranged to visit him at Shoreham.

The shepherd has a treasured sheep-crook made of brass, which he showed me when I went to Shoreham. It belonged to his uncle, Tom Trigwell, and was the first, or one of the first, made, as his uncle's crook was borrowed by the maker of the brass crook for a pattern.

I had heard of these brass crooks several times, and only three weeks before I had found that Mr. Wooler of Pyecombe knew the maker. I experienced a thrill of satisfaction as I handled this specimen. It is well made and nicely finished and must have been a pretty thing in use in the fold. It is figured in the special chapter on crooks.

Mr. Trigwell was born at Hove in 1851. He is noted for his broad smile. His keen sense of humour makes him an entertaining companion, and I was kept amused by his reminiscences of people and quaint incidents. When I asked about smocks he said: " Yes, I always wore one, and a billy-cock hat like I wear now. My uncle Tom wore a smock too. He was a rare man for ' rape greens,' and when he picked a mess of greens to take home (the usual shepherd's allowance) he used to tumble them into his round frock as he picked them." The shepherd's smile broadened at the thought of him. " Him and his greens ! " he exclaimed. " Once I was ready to go home —and glad to go too, for it was miserable old weather. ' Come on, Uncle,' I said, ' I'm ready ! ' ' Stop minute ! ' he says, ' I ent got my greens yet ! ' Diddun matter how miserable a day 'twas he wouldn't go without his greens ! "

The mention of rape greens reminded me of Findon Fair, where another shepherd had praised a big variety of kale with thick stems as sheep food. Mr. Trigwell agreed, in his own quaint way. " Of course they like good food," he said, " they're only like we ! We don't want a bit of apple peel or orange peel—we like the fruit ! "

He told me two little tales of his Uncle Tom, who was a well-known shepherd fifty years ago. One of them also includes Shepherd Clem, famous among all his friends at that date for his extraordinary appetite. Tom Trigwell and Clem once dined, at fair time, at an inn where an excellent half-crown dinner was provided.

As they left they saw a woman selling penny pies, and more in joke than in earnest Tom said to Clem: "I'll pay for all the pies you can eat after all that dinner, Clem!" At once Clem started, and ate thirty pies, a feat which emptied the basket. Tom had to pay the half-crown, and was rather vexed. When the woman offered to go and get another stock of pies from home he refused to wait, and cried: "Good Lord, *no!*— doänt get him any more, missus!—he'd eat more, an' then eat the basket, but I reckon he's had enough!"

The other tale was an account of how three "roughs" were paid in their own coin. In explanation Mr. Trigwell said that the Downs were not as safe at one time as they are now. There were more "rough characters" about, who would choose quiet spots to pay off old scores or "play pranks at someone else's expense, just for devilment."

Tom's son happened to stop at an inn on the Lewes road, Brighton, one Saturday night, and while in the bar he overheard three young men discussing their programme for Sunday. "Let's go up Moulscombe Barn, an' give t' ol' shepherd a roustin'," said one of them, and the others agreed. Little did they suspect that their plans would be known!

Tom was surprised when his son said: "Wake me to-morrow morning, I'm coming up to the barn," but he did so, and while on the way learned of the plot and planned a surprise for the visitors.

In due course the three men appeared and entered the fold. It was just after lambing time, and the shepherd had plenty to do to fill the cages with hay. The dog was tied up, and near to him was a pile of straw, under which Tom's son was hidden. "The men messed about, looking at things," said Mr. Trigwell, "and Tom went on hayin', an' went on hayin', an' went on hayin' till they started their mischief. Then he told them to go." This was the moment they had been waiting for, and what the end would have been nobody knows, but Tom shut the door of the fold and stood at bay with his back to it, holding his hay prong. "Very well," he called, "if you wunt go out you shall stop in." At this moment his son emerged from the straw. "Come to give the old shepherd a rousting, have you?" he remarked, and he untied the dog. The men, taken by surprise, retreated to one side of the yard, but when the dog heard the order "turn 'em back," he obeyed instantly and they were forced to run. The shepherd repeated the order "turn 'em back" till the dog had worried them well and nipped them by the breeches; then he called off the dog and opened the door. He did not have to speak again. The men raced to the door and darted through and disappeared, and the shepherd was not bothered any more.

Mr. Trigwell told me of the old days at the fairs, when flocks were taken thither a day in advance. Shepherds met at an inn at night, a room being reserved for them. On these occasions there was plenty of merriment, and "colt-shoeing" was performed. "Colts" were young men whose experience of shearing was limited to one or two seasons. The man appointed caught each one as he entered, lifted one of his feet and pretended to shoe him. The "colt" was then expected to stand treat to the rest by buying half a gallon of beer.

With jokes and tales and reminiscences the time passed quickly. Mrs. Trigwell called me to take a cup of tea, and I was shown a beautiful photograph of Mr. Trigwell taken at Shoreham. My adjective brought comment from the shepherd. He remarked drily: "Well! 'tis the first time anybody has called *me* beautiful!"

Before I left, the shepherd promised to leave the brass crook to me in his will. Meanwhile, he lent it to me to take a picture of it. We parted with another merry jest, and the first man's face that I met in the street seemed to me a very miserable one after my interview with the old shepherd with his broad smile.

## FRANK UPTON

On the farm known for many years as "Brown's Farm," at West Blatchington I found Mr. Frank Upton, a well-known Sussex shepherd. He is one of the old school. His father and grandfather were both born at Southernham, near Lewes, and both were shepherds, consequently his own training was thorough. Like most old shepherds he dislikes modern ways, and as I chatted with him our conversation naturally drifted to a comparison of the present day with the happier days of the past.

"You can't help noticing the difference wherever you go," he said. "Why, I remember when I could stand on the highest mountain in this part and see twenty flocks of sheep! There was plenty of work for the shearing gangs in those days," he said, "and plenty of good fleeces piled in that barn. The wool buyer used to come and offer so much a pound for them. Now prices are much higher. Old Mr. Brown once said to me: 'If I can be sure of thirty shillings each for my ewes I know I am making them pay me.' Now farmers say that sheep don't pay, yet they get bigger prices for sheep and lambs at the sales, and bigger prices for wool, and sheep don't eat more now than they did then, and their wool grows by itself the same as our hair do! The shepherd's wages don't amount to much—they never did!—so there must be something wrong somewhere! It is the ways of people now that is wrong. Farming wants method as well as work!"

Mr. Upton has a good memory for details of West Blatchington farm in the old days under John Brown, for he has been shepherd there since 1883—fifty years.

"We had no cows then," he said. "Mr. Brown only kept one for milk—he didn't believe in mixing cows and sheep. We used to have about 750 breeding ewes and 300 tegs here. His other farms were at Patcham, Standean, Ditchling, and Rottingdean, and between them all he had always about 5000 breeding ewes. In those days the shepherd was in charge—why! if a shepherd couldn't take full charge of the flocks he wasn't a shepherd at all! John Brown would say: 'Well, Upton, what about this, or that?' and it was soon settled! *Now* I mind these few tegs! I am just about to fold them—fold them on this stuff, sanfoin, not fit to fold on yet! How *can* they get a proper feed?"

The next minute he said: "Oh, well, I've had *my* time and I've known the good old days and remember them! Our work was well done, and we just enjoyed Fair times! We used to have three days for Lindfield Fair—one to take the sheep and leave them; the next day we arranged the pens and so on, and afterwards we had a cricket match at Slug's Wash. Next day was Fair Day, and we came home after the sale.

"Fancy farmers giving shepherds a day off for cricket nowadays!" he exclaimed. "Why, we only have sheep sales instead of fairs—there and back in a day, though *I* don't do it now—Albe does that—for I was seventy yesterday.

"Lindfield Fair was on the 5th August at one time," he said, "but as it sometimes happened to be Bank Holiday and it wasn't easy for people to get there it was changed to the 8th. Lewes Fair," he added, "was always on the 21st September, and all us shepherds used to buy our clothes that day and we used to meet in the evening at 'The Swan,' Southover. If you could have seen inside there you would have found plenty of shepherds!"

Mr. Upton pointed to high ground near the Dyke

road and said: "Years ago you could stand up there and look all round these slopes and see teams of oxen working. It was reg'lar picturesome!—it was the real old Sussex! Now, to us older men, 'tisn't like Sussex at all!" He then pointed to a long shed. "At one time there were twelve oxen kept in that stable," he remarked. "Every year two were sold off and two new ones brought in. Now, take hurdles and wattles," he continued. "Every year we had enough new wattles for a fold. That kept the supply going, you see. They were good oak wattles then, with iron bolts and rings, and lasted well. When I found one defective in any way I was supposed to put it by, and it was taken to the farm workshop and repaired. Iron tops and bolts were made good, and so we had no trouble when pitching. Method, you see! method in everything!"

In his quaint way the shepherd supplied the explanation of the present situation. In former days shepherds were consulted. Now they are ordered. Whereas they were once expected to say what they would require for the sheep they are now expected to bring flocks into condition on what is provided, which is not always an easy matter. Formerly only sheep suitable for the locality were purchased; now any sheep is expected to thrive anywhere and bring a profit in due course.

I told Mr. Upton of my wish to include his reminiscences in my book and explained the outline of it. His interest was proved by immediate action, for under strict conditions he lent me a wonderful portrait of his grandfather, taken at Hailsham. The photograph, on glass tinted by hand, was carefully copied by Messrs. Loader & Sons of Worthing. It is valuable as a record of the costume of the period, and is figured in the chapter on shepherd's clothes.

I have a treasured possession—a genuine old Pyecombe crook, made by Berry, which was given to me by Mr. Upton some years ago. Now, owing to his further kindness, I share his chief treasure and family heirloom—the charming picture of an old Sussex shepherd of a hundred years ago.

## WILLIAM DULY

Half of the September day had passed when I arrived at East Dean to seek for William Duly. I followed directions given me, but when I reached the top of a hill and scanned the valley and the opposite slope there was no sign of sheep or shepherd. Fortunately I met a lady who knew him, and she showed me where his fold was hidden away on a slope beyond the side of a cornfield through which I had passed. Satisfied to know that my forty-mile journey had not been in vain I followed the track to the fold, and found the shepherd just finishing his dinner. The quiet interval provided an excellent opportunity to tell him about the shepherds' book, to obtain a photograph of him and to enjoy a short chat.

Mr. Duly was born at Alciston in 1858. He comes from an old Sussex family. His grandfather and his great-grandfather were both shepherds, and several of the family followed the same employment; consequently his ways are old ways and he is convinced that his type must inevitably die out in due course. I suggested that the large fold he had to pitch was quite enough for him, but he made light of it. "Flocks are not what they were," he said, "and won't be again. Farmers are putting down too much ground—at least a lot of it isn't put down," he added, drily, "it is left to *tumble* down, and the sheep have to eat the rubbish !"

The shepherd attributed all the changes to the death of the old Sussex farmers. He compared several well-known men with the farmers of the past. "They have money," he remarked, "and they have so many acres, but they know no more about real farming than my dog

"A HUNDRED YEARS AGO"
(See interview with Frank Upton in "Some Typical Shepherds")

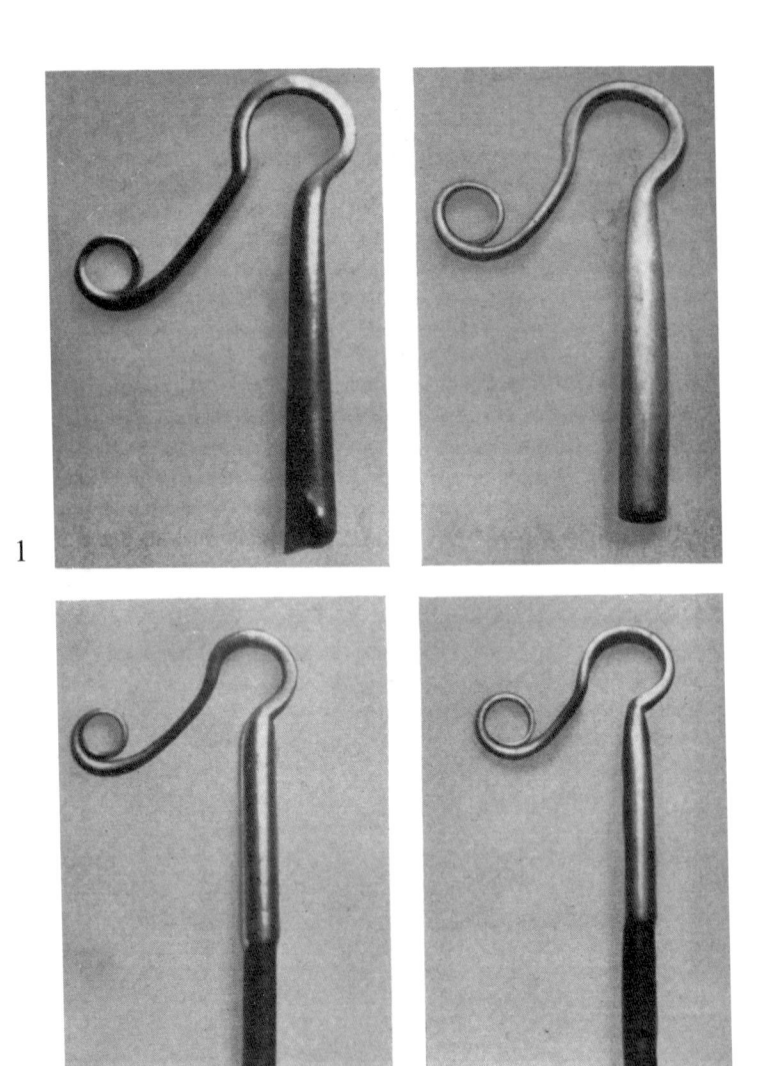

*Photos by the Author*

## SHEEP-CROOKS

1. A crook of the famous old pattern made by Berry of Pyecombe.
2. The first brass crook made in Sussex. 3. Crook made by Green of

does." He reeled off names of many old farmers, including John Brown of West Blatchington, Richard Brown of Lewes, old Mr. Brown of Friston Place, Mr. Hart of Beddingham, Mr. Saxby of West Firle, and Mr. Madgwick of Alciston. Like many more old shepherds he has a wide knowledge of the farms of the district and the changes that have occurred. (It seems a pity that knowledge of such things which these men have cannot be recorded for future reference.)

We spoke of umbrellas, but he does not consider them of much use on East Dean hills owing to strong winds. He said: " A good coat is better, but we can't get the old white overcoats now like we used to buy at Lewes. *They* were the things to keep you dry! The first day I had one the rain fell all day long, but when I took it off I was dry, although the coat was a rare weight with the wet.

"Those coats used to be made by a woman," he continued, "and the seams were not machined like they were in the last one I had. She used two needles and made a very strong watertight seam." The price of a white coat was about 32s. 6d. Some farmers provided one for their shepherd so that he should not be prevented from tending or doing what was necessary on rainy days. At that time he also used to wear the round black hats, known as " parsons' hats " or " chummeys," which he also bought at Lewes. As will be seen from the picture Duly was wearing " false tongues " on his boots. His leggings were lying with his dinner-bag.

Mr. Duly has a love for canister bells. He had a " ring " of twenty-one, but it is now incomplete. " I sold one to an artist," he said. " I didn't want to, but he was so persuasive that at last I let him have one. After that I lost some among thick heather, and that spoilt the ring."

My reference to the two dogs in the fold led the

shepherd to chat about them. He prefers bob-tails or rough-haired dogs to collies as he has found them better for work. He said that where the feeding-ground is bordered by crops a bob-tail will watch and see that the sheep do not intrude over the border line, but he has not found that collies do this so well. Bob-tails may feel the heat as much as most dogs, but they disregard cold and wet and work through it, whereas a collie will endeavour to take shelter from drenching rain under the shepherd's big coat or some other cover.

The shepherd's leisure time came to an end. My long return journey did not allow a wait until evening for another chat and so we parted. I was rewarded for my trip by such a pleasant interview and by a little picture of the shepherd, and although it is only an enlargement from a "fool-proof" film, a friend recognised the figure with the crook immediately. "Ah! I know that one!" he said; "that is the old shepherd at East Dean, named Duly!"

## GEORGE BAILEY

Miss I. A. Battye, of Kensington, sent me a little picture of a shepherd whom she met in the Steyning district. I had not met him, so took the photo to the old shop in Steyning where horn lanterns and old-fashioned things were once obtained by some of the Sussex shepherds. Mr. Rice of the shop at once said: "That is George Bailey of Beeding Court Farm," and so I picked up the clue I wanted.

I found that Mr. Bailey had retired from regular work, the flock being in charge of his nephew, Mr. Bazen. He was out when I called to see him and I arranged to go again after a ramble, but after climbing a steep lane I chanced to hear the voices of sheep, and on mounting a bank saw Mr. Bailey and his nephew in a fold. They posed for their portraits, and later I followed Mr. Bailey to his home for a chat.

The old shepherd was born in 1856. He arrived in Sussex from Wiltshire when only three years old, and after moving about here and there with his father (also a shepherd), settled at Myrtle Grove for some time. From there he came to Beeding Court Farm, where he stayed for forty-six years. Though no longer "the shepherd," he still drifts to the fold, as one might expect, for the sheep are his chief interest.

Mr. Bailey has vivid recollections of the old harvest suppers, shearings, fairs, and other notable events. He looked forward to the fairs. "There were three 'lamb fairs,'" he said, "St. John's, Findon (July), and Horsham, and three big fairs, Lindfield, Findon (September), and Lewes.

"The old shearing gangs were great boys," he remarked. "There was the Bury gang, the Steyning gang, the Fulking gang and the Clapham gang. Their numbers were not always exactly the same, but usually about sixteen or eighteen. Some were very fond of their beer, and there was some rough play among them at times, but still they were great boys, and I have had plenty of fun watching them when they came at shearing." He looks back now, with amusement, on some of the incidents connected with shearers and their beer, and related some of them to me.

His tale of a sheep-washing gang is recorded in the notes on that subject.

I asked Mr. Bailey about smocks. He always used to wear them, and bought them at Lewes. His last one came to an untimely end. He had a big fire-place in the room used as a temporary home in lambing time. His mate, before leaving, made up a big fire and left it for him, but in the meantime the flames caught more than they were supposed to. Much was destroyed, including his smock.

The shepherd gave me an old black umbrella, bought

at Lewes. He has had green ones, but those came from Storrington. He still has his shears in an old pouch. The latter is an exceptional specimen; the thick leather point has a farthing on each side held by a rivet.

Mr. Bailey has followed his father's ways, and is skilled in animal cutting. I saw his flat metal stretcher and two searing irons. They have had a lot of use. Only the night previous to my visit a farmer from a distance had asked for his services, but he does not feel that he can tackle big animals any more. I appreciated the shepherd's remarks. He reminded me that the rearing of domestic animals brings the necessity for a number of rather cruel operations, and that, because it is not a cheerful subject for discussion or comment in the ordinary way, it is not generally remembered. His sympathy for the animals is strong, and he is content to know that his skill in dealing with them has saved many from prolonged and unnecessary pain.

"A shepherd's life," said Mr. Bailey, "is full of anxiety. You never know what may happen in the few hours you may be away from the sheep. They may be frightened or they may break loose, find wrong feed, get blown out and die before you go back! I have had all sorts of experiences," he said, "but the worst thing of all to a shepherd is to be with a farmer who will not feed the flock. Once, long ago, I called a farmer's attention to some sheep and told him they wanted hay. 'Hay!' he said, ''tis only November!—they don't want hay; they're all right!' So there 'twas! Well, I went on for another week, and then I said: 'You'll lose some if you don't send some hay up.' He came to see them again. 'My! they look bad,' he said. 'You shall have some hay.' After a few more days he sent a little, but by then several had died.

"It would save such a lot of bother," said Mr. Bailey. "if farmers would allow their shepherds to know what is best for the sheep." His remark was simply and quietly made, but his gentleness only seemed to emphasize the sincerity which prompted it. It seemed a matter for regret that such an observation was considered necessary by one who had spent his life in the service of Sussex flocks.

## SHEPHERD Z

For a long time I had known of Shepherd Z through using a certain footpath through a farm—a big, bony old fellow, slow of step and slow of speech. He would reply shortly if spoken to, but not otherwise, and his big, grave, wrinkled face was as expressionless as that of any sheep he tended.

One day as we met at a gateway two rough-looking men appeared from behind me. "Hullo, Shepherd!" cried one, "is this the path for Burpham?" To my surprise the old man drawled—"Yes, 'tis, an' you *know* 'tis!" The men made some caustic remarks, but walked off immediately. "Took me for a fool!" drawled the old shepherd, "they thought I diddun know 'em again! They asked me the same thing 'bout two year ago! They be up to no good; *they* don't want go Burpham!" Immediately he went away through the turnips to his fold.

Months afterwards a man said to me: "I should think old Green at Hilldown Farm could tell you a lot for your book if you could get him to talk, although he won't talk to me!" (I found that he was referring to old Z, but had mixed up names of shepherds and farms.) I therefore lay in wait for the shepherd one morning as he led his flock to a pond. The sheep raced by him up a sunken path in their anxiety to reach the water. "They be quicker'n I be!" he said, as I met him and spoke, "but I used be quick 'nough at one time!"

When the sheep were watered he relapsed into his usual curious mood, but permitted me to walk to the fold. Once the sheep were safely penned he brightened a little. I was surprised to learn that his age was sixty-five years. I should have guessed it to be seventy-five at least.

"I diddun mean to be shepherd at sixty-five," he said wistfully, as he gazed into space. "When I was twenty I went to Hampshire to join the Army, but I diddun pass, so I comed back an' started again." After a pause he remarked: "My idea was to join up for twenty-one years—by that time I should have known whether I liked it or not; anyway I expect I should have seen a bit of the world, but I'm sixty-five now, and except for my day at Hampshire I haven't seen anywhere but Sussex!"

I asked about his crook. Was it an old one? He didn't know! He told me, without enthusiasm, that he had it from another shepherd forty years ago and had used it ever since. Mention of other matters aroused no interest in this extraordinary man. No anecdote, no information, no opinion rewarded me for my long walk. I might just as well have tried to catechise the sheep-dog, although the man's reputation for incessant efficient work was vouched for by another shepherd—a fact which seemed to indicate that a flock was his one interest. The memory of his trip to another county appeared to be the only important thing in his life—the wonder of what he *might* have been and *might* have seen had lasted for forty-five years! He had smiled when he told me about it, so it was not ill-humour that could account for his peculiar way. It was not sourness, not melancholy—merely an apparent indifference to ordinary matters. Perhaps some vague unsatisfied longing to "see the world" had crushed him! Who can tell?

I sat on the turf afterwards and wrote my notes—this record of my only disappointing interview with an old shepherd; yet the journey to see him was not without result, for it added to my gallery of mental pictures one of a most unusual type.

The following pages describe three meetings with shepherds, and are typical of many records made in my note-books after downland rambles. These appeared in *Downland Treasure*, and are reprinted by kind permission of Messrs. Methuen and Co., Ltd.

I

What a treat are those occasional wonderful winter days that help us through the weeks of uncomfortable weather!—days when sudden spells of sunshine invite us to linger in the lee of a sheltered bank or hedgerow. I had tramped to one of my favourite Downland haunts and found a warm corner among a clump of stunted thorns, furze, and rough herbage, and stood there watching a blackbird and a stonechat searching in their own particular ways for something to appease their hunger.

From a deep valley beyond the ploughed ground in front of me a muffled sound of bells floated up; but the haze, which the sun had not quite dispersed, hid the flock from sight. Presently, as the mist lifted, I suddenly spied a few sheep with the sunlight shining on them, and a moment later the shepherd came into view, waving his crook, for his keen eyes had noticed me at once.

We met among the furrows, and were soon discussing many topics. As we doddled along his big collie followed us; then, as we halted a minute, he sat down to wait. Suddenly his ears were raised and his body quivered. His imploring glance at the shepherd's face was enough. His master " clucked " once (as one would do to start a horse) and away sped the dog over the furrows. Two eyes, keener than my own, saw a rabbit in the distance, but two ears, keener than our four put together, had heard the pitiful squeal as a stoat had pounced on his victim. " Come on ! " cried the shepherd; his pace was wonderful as he made for the rabbit, while the dog gave all his attention to his unsuccessful chase of the stoat. By the time I reached my friend he had picked up the rabbit, which was as though mesmerized. It did not struggle, but sat as a stuffed creature in his hands, its body taut, its eyes fixed. The dog returned, and seeing the rabbit, reached up and washed its face with his tongue. Still the poor dear did not move. " She be done for," said the shepherd, as I stroked the rabbit's head. " Ef I putt her down, Mus' Stoat'd soon fin' her again. 'Tis often the way! " So saying, he turned away and, with one quick dexterous movement, he finished the stoat's work. " I bean't 'lowed to take a rabbit," he said, " but I reckon as 'tis a pity to leave 'im for Mus' Stoat or Mas'r Fox, so I'll hide 'un for ye till ye be ready to goo." He turned homewards shortly after, leaving me in charge of the flock while he dined.

My team were no trouble. They headed the right way and the bells kept up a merry, tuneful jingle. I placed my lunch on the turf of a little mound and stood as I eat, noting the sounds of the bells. I would rather lay my food on the thyme-scented turf than on a dirty plate, although some folks are not so fussy.

A magpie sailed by; he quickened his pace as he caught sight of a stranger in his domain. Presently I followed the shepherd home, and having reported that the flock were making for the right hill, I shared his pot of tea. Soon he picked up his coat and crook, and with the collie in attendance we crossed to some ground where he had noted a few worked flints. On the way I picked up an old ox-shoe from a rut with four nails still in it, and as we reached the flinting ground I found one good specimen.

The collie grew impatient. He looked very disgusted when his master said: " Be quiet, ye monkey! " and was not satisfied until we moved on and reached the rough grass and bushes. Here he caught sight of his old

## SOME TYPICAL SHEPHERDS

enemy once more. " Cluck ! " went the shepherd's tongue, for he had seen the stoat too ; but though the dog raced off at the command the agile creature escaped again. Then a beautiful " longtail " rose just in front of us and sped away to some trees over the valley. " 'Twur ju's here that he killed a pheasan'," said my companion. With twinkling eyes he continued : " He diddun' know as he was wrong till I telled him so an' putt the pheasan' in me pocket ! T'missus stuffed 'un an' cooked 'un, an' I had half of 'un for brakfus' an' t'other half for supper, for she doan' like pheasan'. I had a reg'lar good feed thet day, so I did ! "

As we doddled about, slowly following the sheep, the shepherd pointed out a track made by a fox as he ran along a furrow. " Reckon I'd like to meet he," he said, " for I know a man as'd give fifteen shillin's for his jacket." He fumbled about in his pocket. " Here's somethin' for ye," he remarked, and produced five fox teeth. " I foun' two in one place an' three in another," he told me.

As the sunlight began to wane the air turned chilly. " 'Tis time to turn 'em back," explained the shepherd, as we altered our course, and we started to round up the odd members of the flock, who had strayed into quiet spots among thick herbage and furze-bushes. " Better jes' give a look over this brow an' mek' sure," said my friend ; and we did so. We flushed a brace of partridges, and each one dropped a small wing feather, which floated to our feet ; but no more sheep were found, so we stood for a minute viewing the scene before us.

The green track in the deep valley was deserted, but on the hill-side below the next brow were two men busy at a rabbit bury. " There be ole Mike," said the shepherd ; " bet ye I mek' him tark to me ! " So saying he put his big palm to the side of his mouth and shouted : " Putt ye head down t'hole, an' stop 'em frum comin'

out!" The big voice reverberated in the still air.
Instantly the reply came across the two hundred yards
stretch like a clear distant voice on a telephone: "I
c'd do thet an' all. I bean't like some, got 'ead as 'ud
fill a bucket!"

The rabbit-catcher must have heard our burst of
laughter. The shepherd shook as he chuckled. "I telled
ye, diddun I?" he gasped. "I telled ye! I ketch 'un
every time! Reckon all they rabbits be reg'lar froughten'
wi' him shoutin', but he can't kip quiet ef you speaks
first, an' his tongue is allus ready wi' a good answer for
ye!" His laughter bubbled out again and again, and
lasted until we reached the fold. Here I left the lonely
couple who work together for the good of the flock,
who converse by secret signs and understand one another
so well. "Allus pleased to see ye," said the shepherd as
we parted; and as if to endorse his statement the collie
thrust his nose into my hand. I stopped by a stack to
pick up a long, slim bundle. I disposed of it in the
correct manner, and nobody suspected from my appearance
that I had a bunny for a companion.

My friend has a hard life, and is the victim of every
kind of cruel weather; yet inside him is that germ which
can only flourish in the open air. Every mark and track
is a message to him. The rustle of a bolting rabbit, the
swish of a flushed game-bird's wings, and the song of his
treasured bells mean so much to him that he needs no
newspaper to amuse him. I believe that if he were confined
among bricks and mortar in the town he would
soon pine away.

2

As I made my way into Downland on the sixth of
November the sun drove away the mist. The magician
lured out a Red Admiral and many flies. It made high-
lights appear on the haws and accentuated the remarkable

difference in colour of those on two adjoining bushes—one lot a deep crimson and the other lot almost scarlet.

In the sheltered lane a few late blackberries lingered, not juicy as those of last month, but excellent fare for the pink-breasted bullfinch which dipped down from a bush and vanished behind the hedge. One stray dandelion was a welcome sight; so was the magpie that sat on the topmost spray of a young tree and only noticed me in time to dive off and hurry over the field to a distant brow. I allowed three men with a terrier to pass along in front and waited about so that I might not miss the sight of any of my winged friends.

I found old David the shepherd near the top of the hill. I had been busy looking at many things and watching skylarks, and had not noticed him until he waved his crook. His little, rather bent figure, clothed in drab, weather-worn garments, his ancient hat, the shaggy grey and white bob-tail and the thickly fleeced team were so much a part of the hill and blended so well with the tall, dried-up grass among which they stood that it was no wonder I had not seen them before.

This shepherd does not usually care to converse much, but he does not mind my visits, for I never outstay my welcome. "Mornin'," he said, in his usual sharp way, as I approached. "Well, shepherd," I replied, "I did not expect to find you as far from home as this." "Oh, yes," said the old man, "I shall be 'bout here for the rest of t'year, I 'spect."

"You don't have many visitors here?" I queried. "Far too many for me!" was his sharp reply. I glanced at him quickly, and he saw me do so. "Oh, I doan't mind *you* comin'," he said, "but those people with dogs be a noosance on the downs. There be three men not long gone by with a tarrier dog; *they'll* hev to be telled to kip to the path next, an' as for thet great beast as just passed you a-comin' along, I reckon I'd shoot 'im!"

For once the old man waxed warm and chatted. " I reckon ninety-nine dogs out of ivry hundred should be shot," he continued, " and after thet I'd shoot a few more. They bean't no use, you know ; they be only a damned noosance to other people, an' as for beastes like that great big 'un, 'tis wickid to kip 'em. Do you know this," he said, as he bent forward and half rested his chin on the crook head, " thet dog costes nigh twelve shillin's a week to feed ! A pound o' beef steak every day, an' bread an' milk, an' what not ! All good food as'd feed a fam'ly o' children ! I calls it damned wickid, so I doos. 'Tis more wickider than swearin', for swearin' you can unnerstan'—'tis on'y a few silly words—but sich waste is downright wickid. It doan't do anybody any good 'cept t' butcher ! Twelve shillin's a week ! Why, 'twas my wages one time, an' see what I did with it ! Thet boarhound beast ain't worth it, an' you know I'm right ! " He had stated his case so plainly that I could only agree with him.

Cluck-cluck, clong-clong, sang the old bells on the sheep. " You have only a few bells on ! " I remarked. " Yes," he replied, " an' quite enough too ! I doan't care for these tin cans. The boss has a tubful at home an' I hope he'll kip 'em there. I doan't want 'em all round me. Now, my father's latten bells was music. A set there was, the shape of a cup upside down, an' most of 'em little 'uns, but they was a band o' music an' no mistake ! "

The shepherd changed his position, and by the way he grasped his crook I knew it was a signal to move. " Well, I must be going," I said. " Good-bye," said the old man, " you've got a smartish walk home if you be goin' home to dinner. Reckon we shall hev a drop o' rain presently, though 'tis bright now," and he and the shaggy dog moved slowly after the flock.

### 3

On the thirteenth of March I set out in my usual style to seek for beauty and romance across the country-side. The wonderful early morning light gave a peculiar brightness to the colour effects, as I passed furrowed fields and sown fields separated by faintly tinted hedges and lines of elms. The latter were already beautiful at a distance, with that elusive blush of smoky pink which appears to wrap their branches before the bloom actually gives the trees a distinct colour. Smoke from the chimney of a thatched cottage appeared as a blue vapour as it wreathed and ascended and faded away among some elm branches. Rooks were much in evidence; so were their companions the gulls. One becomes accustomed to seeing gulls inland as well as on the shore.

I did not find the shepherd I sought where his lambing fold was pitched last time, and on enquiry learned that he was yet another mile away. It was no hardship to do an extra mile—such a mile!—with countless things to see. First another shepherd's family of horned sheep whose white babies were capering and prancing as only lambs can do; next a sallow bush with buds of silver; then a party of chaffinches, not yet disbanded for the nesting season; then a patch of ivy of wonderful beauty, tinted with crimson colour. Interest without end!—hazel catkins above, dog's mercury below, and, lower still, hart's-tongue ferns in the ditch; a robin, a rabbit, a startled ringdove flapping, a clump of speedwell blossoms, a weasel, a bunch of cattle grazing, and a baby holly tree showing among some withered grasses. A tomtit was perched on the post of a farm gate, calling with shrill, sawing note, and warning me that there was no admittance that way, as a printed notice stated. He did not know that I was a privileged person with a passport to the ancient barn in the distance.

As I made my way toward the dike-bounded fields I could see hurdles in a mangold patch, and found the fold tenanted by a number of ewes and babies. Even to my eyes they appeared a somewhat poor lot of Southdowns, and it was not until I met the shepherd that I knew the reason for their draggled appearance.

"You be thinkin' things 'bout they fine lot Southdowns, reckon!" said the man with the crook dryly as we met. "Come down t'barn an' see the rest of 'em!" On the way he told me how one of the dikes into which the yard drained had become dammed by a fallen bank. This caused the water to wash back into the yard, and as the reason for the trouble could not be traced at once, the place was soon flooded. It was saddening to listen to the account of the poor ewes waiting to lamb with water washing round them, and of newly born lambs in the same plight till they could be rescued. It took a long time to move over three hundred sopped ewes from the straw litter. A scout was sent out, who reported that the dike was clear and the sluice clear; consequently it was not until the shepherd himself left everything to search about that the fallen bank was discovered. The scout's ears must have burned when the shepherd spoke of him to me; but there was excuse for hasty words, for although by the time I arrived the water had receded and the place had been re-littered, the sad results of the catastrophe were still apparent.

In the ordinary course of events the stately old barn would have formed a perfect setting for a model fold. The main building, with its big old doors, through which the corn was carried in bygone days, faces the north, and the east and west "wings," with a connecting wall, enclose a yard only separated from the sea by one long field. This sun-trap was arranged for the main lambing fold. Inside the wings were rows of pens, now mostly occupied by ewes with their sons and daughters; but there were many mangers fitted with chains, and the shepherd informed me that the barn was mostly used to house fat bullocks. Just now the mangers were filled with fresh straw and fodder, which the good farmer had rushed down with all possible speed, while piles of roots and hay were stored in the centre of the big barn.

The shepherd gave me a surprise. He opened a connecting door, and there, in a temporary stall, was a cow, to provide the necessary milk for so many bottle babies and weak ewes. It was the first time I had seen a cow installed for this purpose.

It was only when we made a tour of inspection round the pens that I realized how deeply the shepherd was affected by the upset. Some of his sheep had been with him two years, some three; now a number of them were dead and many ailing, while many of the first lambs were born to a life of hours only, after all the months of care which had been expended on the ewes. The shepherd remarked on each pen in turn. " This ol' lady lost her lamb! " " This 'un had two—on'y one left now! " " Two more for t'bottle—no milk, you see! " " Here be 'nother! If I get her over to-night she'll live." " This un's bad! I've done all I can, but she'll go out, reckon! " And so on. A weary list indeed, only softened by the endearing phrases whispered to each patient in turn, which I was not supposed to notice. The poor man seemed quite crushed by his misfortune, for this little flood, not worth a newspaper paragraph as news, was as bad to him as a shipwreck.

We worked round to the centre again and my friend cut up many roots in generous slices. As these fell into a large trug placed on a wheelbarrow a soft " Moo! " sounded through the partition. " All right, Pansy. I hear ye!" he called, and in due course the gentle cow received her midday meal (and a caress as well), after which he led the way to his hut, where the stove needed stoking in readiness for the warming of the milk on which so many frail lives depended. Here I left my friend to his duties, for somehow I felt that I could not intrude upon the patient efforts of a beaten men who would not yet own defeat.

I set out this morning to seek for beauty, and found it in the elms, the smoke, the silver sallows, the crimson ivy, and all the rest. I also found sorrow—hard and crushing sorrow; yet in the shepherd's tender devotion to his poor unfortunate family surely there was beauty too!

*Those who have listened to Dr. Habberton Lulham's lectures will recall many of his quaint and delightful stories of inhabitants of the countryside. At first we are inclined to think that he must have had unique opportunities to note such items and to use his camera to such good purpose, but as we listen we realize that his boundless enthusiasm, and sympathy with his subject, is responsible for the collection of stories and pictures that please us so much.*

*Dr. Lulham has known many shepherds, and when he told me the appealing tale of Henry Rewell, and described his first meeting with my friend Darkie Funnell of Wilmington, I wished to include these and other incidents with my own records. With characteristic kindness he showed his interest by giving welcome assistance in several ways and by contributing the following chapter.—B. W.*

## STRAY MEMORIES

I RESPOND with pleasure to the author's invitation to add a chapter to this excellent record of South Down shepherds, and feel the opportunity a privilege.

For many a year I have counted certain of these men among my valued friends, finding very much to admire in their kindly nature, their efficiency, their wholehearted, and often self-denying, devotion to their duties, and their general good sense and intelligence.

It would seem that their many hours of solitude on the hill-tops has raised their thoughts more than a little out of the common ruck and made them, in their own way, wise, or as we in Sussex say, " perusing " old men. I recall a Polonius of the sheepfold whose mind was a storehouse of homely wisdom and precept: " Now hark'ee, my lad," he would say to his boy help, " mind as you allus keeps better company than what you be yerself! And look'ee—if Youth could know what Age'll crave, how many a sixpence Youth'd save ! " Many of his bits of advice and criticisms were spiced with humour. " There, Jim," he'd say, " I'm afeared 'tis no good me trying to knock any sense into that stoopid wooden head o' yours ; but put yer cap on, me boy, and pull it down quick—there's a woodpecker a-comin' ! "

A late Vicar of Ditchling used to tell of an old shepherd whose wise sayings he stored and valued. One summer a London visitor to the village said : " Well, shepherd, it's nice enough here in summer, but it must be a miserable place when these lanes are deep in winter mud." " Well, yes, sir," shepherd replied, "'tis true we do all have to walk through the mud—but some of us looks at the stars." Another day, after he had paid his only visit to London and had by chance seen some pageant of the streets—a Lord Mayor's Show, I think it was—the Vicar said: "I suppose, Ben, you never in all your life saw anything so wonderful"; and, after a pause, the answer came: "Yes, sir, I have; I've seen dawn come up over the Downs."

The minds of these old shepherds (I speak of them as "old," for to-day, alas, fewer and fewer young men care to carry their fathers' crooks after them) are often surprisingly open to new ideas. Some years ago I suggested to one of them, who was losing ewes at lambing-time from a puerperal infection, that it would, I thought, be a wise thing to dip his hands in a pail of antiseptic solution before handling them. He at once saw the point and acted on it, with benefit to his charges; though, one must add, his master, hearing of my innovation, disapproved of such "new-fangled notions."

Another shepherd friend of mine—Tom Rushbridge, of Wick Farm, Ditchling—had among his sheep, as often happens, a "jumper"; a ewe that will jump any low hedge and get away from the rest of the flock. One day as I sat beside him and his dog on the Downs, his ewes were feeding below us in a long, sickle-shaped line, the lower end of which was near a hedge that divided the open Down from a field of rape, and suddenly one of these "jumpers" leapt over it. "There she goes again," Tom said: " dunnamany times old Bob here ain't turned her out o' that bit o' rape a'ready this marnin', a rare skaddle old hussy she be!" (That's a good old Sussex word, "skaddle," meaning mischievous, tiresome.) But he cured her: he had noticed that before she leapt she always pricked her ears forward—as a hunter does before he takes one over a hedge—and the flock-mark of his sheep being a hole punched through the ear, he took a piece of stout thread and, passing it through the hole, tied it firmly to the wool at the back of her neck, with the result that, being unable to prick her ears, she gave up jumping.

A custom which was once always practised in Downland, and is so still in some villages, is the placing of a lock of sheep's wool on the breast of a shepherd at his burial, so that—Downlanders say—he may be able, on Resurrection Day, to hold it up as proof of the calling which kept him up on the hills and far away from the church on Sundays! When giving a South Down lecture lately in London, my chairman was our witty Lord Chief Justice, Lord Hewart, and, speaking when I had finished, he said: " Apropos of what the doctor was telling us about the lock of sheep's wool, I could not help thinking, as he spoke, that it might perhaps be a good thing for me and many of my friends if we could be buried with a golf-ball on the chest!"

The shepherd's knowledge of individual ewes is surprising, and he not only knows each at a glance, but remembers her history. I heard Tom Rushbridge say, when putting a newly born lamb to its mother: " Here ye are, my dear, and I hopes you'll have better luck with this one than you did last year."

He was one of my most valued shepherd friends, and I have not forgotten his wise words of sympathy on the death of a medical friend of mine who was often on the hills with me and whose absence he had noticed; he ended by saying, " Ah, I had a friend like that once, and I thinks of him most days still."

At that time I used often to go from my cottage to the lambing-yard instead of to bed, taking with me a thermos of hot cocoa for the shepherd, whom I would sometimes find working almost asleep, tired out with the day and night duties of lambing-time—with us the first three weeks of March—when he had scarcely a chance of taking off his clothes. I would go on duty for a few hours, and the shepherd, dropping upon the straw of an empty pen, would instantly fall asleep, and sleep on like a child till I woke him and told him what lambs had been born and what I had done with them.

I look back to such nights as times of great happiness. All around one were the sounds and scents of coming Spring : young lambs calling from the yard, young birds from the thatch, and near by one knew the first flowers were opening. Suddenly, perhaps, a barn-owl, in down-bemuffled flight, would waver across the lambing-yard, looking, in the moonlight, like a piece of blown silver-paper, and, gliding up to the roof-tree, would sit peering down for mice. And above the great shoulder of the sheltering Beacon the stars glittered. Happy, peaceful hours !

As might be expected, the shepherd has many strange ideas and semi-superstitious beliefs. I have heard one tell how sometimes his dog would crouch, looking up and whimpering, because, he said, the witch-hounds were running overhead, hunting some escaping evil spirit back to its doom. Another spoke of what he called " false dawn " when, an hour or so before the true dawn came, a lightening of the eastern sky appeared, a little breeze would spring up, sheep would move about and feed awhile, larks would rise for a short flight and half-hearted faint song, his sleeping dogs would uncurl themselves, stretch their limbs and turn and turn about before settling again. Then the light would fade, the breeze die down, and all rest as before.

Shepherds have told me, too, of strange lambs their ewes have borne, beaked like an owl, or with hare's fur in place of wool, the result, they said, of the ewe having been frightened while carrying her lamb, by what they called a furze-owl (probably the Little Owl) flying out from a bush by which she was feeding, or by a hare suddenly starting from its form beside her.

The lamb with the hare's fur had died, and I asked shepherd what he had done with it, if he had sent it to the Bramber village museum (where, by the by, an extraordinary collection of rare and curious things, and cleverly stuffed, amusing groups of animals and birds may be seen). "No," he said, "my missus took and made me a wery good wesket out o' that skin, she did."

Some of my earliest memories of our shepherds are connected with a bird once very common on the Downs, but now comparatively rare—the wheatear which, fifty years ago, was esteemed a delicacy for the table, and was known as the Sussex Ortolan. The bird has a habit of running into any hole or other shelter, especially at the approach of heavy clouds, and the shepherds, knowing this peculiarity, would cut a great number of small T-shaped trenches on the Downs, a few inches deep, fixing a running noose of horse-hair at the inter-section of the T's two parts, and covering in all but the ends with a turf. Into the trench the bird would run and get caught in the noose, to be sold by the shepherd to poulterers in the Downland towns. This trapping became so common that farmers at last forbade it, as their men were devoting too much time to the trade. Nowadays, though they are no longer trapped, one may see, in a long walk over the Downs, no more than a pair or two of wheatears; nesting, perhaps, a little way within a disused rabbit-burrow.

Jim Fowler was for years shepherd at another Ditchling farm; a good shepherd he was, too, and always ready for a chat, and willing to put his store of experience at one's service. His face, from long exposure to wind and weather, was more deeply lined that that of any man of his age I have seen, but the lines were good lines, and, when he made his humorous remarks, added much to their effect. The picture shows him taking his ewes and lambs off to the hills, with his little boy—now an experienced shepherd himself—beside him; and he appears again in the following picture, where you may imagine him speaking the old shepherd's toast, before drinking from his oaken keg :—

> If I had store,
> By sheep and fold
> I'd give you gold;
> But, since I'm poor,
> By crook and bell
> I wish you well."

Another valued friend was dear old Henry Rewell, who succeeded Rushbridge on Ditchling Beacon, a kindly, wise old man for whom all who knew him seemed to have an affection. He has gone to his last fold, and for me there is something sadly wanting from the hill now I no longer see his bent, but still sturdy form, in its old blue linen jacket, leaning on the long ash pole he carried. In his last years he used this as a support when walking, with both hands on it and holding it across his body, much as a punter holds his pole. His back was very bent, from some old spinal trouble; but, in spite of this, I was told, he used for many years before her death to carry his old wife, morning and night, up and down the steep stairs of their cottage. And he had thought out, a neighbour told me, a clever plan for her comfort during the hours he was away with his sheep : from their table he had cut out a semicircular piece, and in this space he placed an office-chair with a pivoted seat, so that she could sit there and, turning about, reach the various things needed for many little household jobs in his absence.

The reader will perhaps know that if a sheep loses her lamb, and another, which may be in poor condition, has two, the experienced shepherd will often get the bereaved one to act as foster-mother to one of the twins; but this she will sometimes refuse to do unless the skin of her dead lamb is fitted as a jacket to the living, when, recognising the scent of it, she will take its wearer to be indeed her own dear departed. Rewell was particularly skilful in making these little jackets, and in the photograph you see him slipping one on. It was tied round the lamb's throat and kept on for a few days only.

He was very weather-wise, too, and, among many true portents, of which he told me, one was that when the barren ewes skipped and played about of an evening with the lambs it was a sure sign of rain.

His patriarchal appearance was marred in his later days through a piece of advice given him by a lady visitor to his cottage: she had lately shingled her hair and was advising a similar process for everyone she met, and persuaded the old man to take his sheep-shears and cut his fine beard severely across close under his chin, quite spoiling him from my camera's point of view. However, I had already secured many a good picture of him that remind me, now I can no longer find him watching his flock on the hill, or sit chatting by his fire-side, of one of the most lovable characters I have known.

Mr. Barclay Wills told me one day of a particularly picturesque and jolly shepherd, and good fellow generally, known as "Darkie" Funnell, of Wilmington Priory Farm, and, suggested that I should try to secure a photograph of him. So, one fine morning, I started out to do so, and passing through a farm on my way to the hills where I expected to find him with his flock, I noticed some harvesters at work and went into the field to ask on what part of the hill I might find the shepherd. One of the men attracted me by his merry brown face, ear-rings and fine head of white hair. "No," he said, with a twinkling smile, in answer to my inquiry, "I reckon you won't find him on the hill, and I don't suppose you'll come across him anywheres about the farm, but I shouldn't be surprised if you saw him standing here afore ye!" It was "Darkie" himself, and well he repaid my search for him by his pleasant talk as he worked and his obliging posing for some pictures.

The flocks are becoming fewer and fewer on our hills; why, I don't know, for there is unlimited pasturage, a chain of unfailing dew-ponds still, and the small Southdown mutton is as much in request as ever. To give up the hill-flocks seems like throwing away the goodwill of a valuable and old-established business; and no farmer has given me what seemed to be a sufficient reason for doing so, but nevertheless sheep and shepherds are going, more's the pity.

My gossiping must end, and I have, I fear, already allowed my pleasure in these random memories to lead my pen too far. The shepherds may be fewer, but there are still good men to be met and talked with here and there, from Beachy Head to the Hampshire border; and may the day be far distant when their solitary forms are seen no more, and their flocks and the music of their bells cease to lend an added touch of poetry to the beauty of our Downland hills.

Habberton Lulham, in his poem "On the Downs," from which we now quote, after speaking of the Elementals that haunt our hills, says of the shepherd:

> But see, there stands, still in the earthly toils,
> A brother soul, a shepherd of the hills;
> Alone he bides, a tall old man, and leans
> With knotty hands clasping his hazel crook,
> The old, blue cloak, patched, worn and weather-stained,
> Hangs to his leathern leggings; at his feet
> His two dogs lie, and down the hill below,
> In a long sickle-line, the feeding sheep
> Call in a hundred tones and sound their bells—

Hark to the mellow music. Sit by him,
And, silent though he be from many a year
Of hill-side solitudes, yet, as the pine
On yonder crest speaks when the strong wind stirs
Its heart, the breath of sympathy will break
His silentness ; and, wiser than he knows,
He hides a world of curious lore behind
Those weather-beaten eyes. But while his tales
Find their slow, plodding words, a smouldering sun
Sinks through the clouds and purple mist behind
The western hills, whereon its last red arc
Glows for a moment like the watchman's fire
Before some ancient camp. He calls his dogs
And sends them forth ; eager they fly to bring
The wandering sheep together ; as he waves
Them on, his crook's head catches the red light,
And shines as when within that Pyecombe forge,
A hundred years ago, his grandsire watched
A cunning hand beat out its long-thought curves.

   I will go too, and help him pitch the fold
Down by the hazel holt, and strew the lines
Of golden swedes. By darkening lanes we wend
Behind the pattering feet and tinkling bells.

. . . . .

It is the hour now of that wondrous blue
Deep, rich and luminous, old painters used
To drape about their stately dreams of God ;
And now the shepherd's lanthorn shines about
His folded flock, its mellow, orange ray
Making a lovelier, richer blue above
And all around the little ring of light.

   I linger still about the sleeping farm :
Here are the lambs, that start up from their straw
And stare with bright eyes as the lanthorn beams
Above their wattled walls. How soft the moon
Shines on their gentle forms, and throws the shade
Of each small head upon its neighbour's fleece.

And in the farmyard how the whitewashed walls
Glint in its light, and every shadow lies
How richly dark; silvery the old slates gleam,
And dappled with leaf-shadows stand the stacks;
A planet in each puddle shines, and see,
The muddy duck-pond brims with sky and stars.
The homestead's pile of twisted chimneys looks
A fairy castle, with its battlements
And clustering towers; and, where that creeper falls,
A ladder for some elfin escapade
Seems hanging from the turret-window high.
Oh, one may wander all the moonlit night,
Lingering amid the soft, grey silences,
And find, transmuted from dull things of day,
A land of unimagined loveliness.

    And what of ye, dear vision-haunted hills,
To what dream-staple are ye woven now,
By what moon-magic, and the tender aid
Of what aërial alchemy? Your crests
And flowing curves seem melted in the sky,
Dissolved beneath their tides of glimmering dew,
And all your holts and hollows washed away
By stealing clouds and pearly waves of mist.

# THE SHEPHERD'S POSSESSIONS

WHEN we meet a shepherd tending his flock on the downs we may notice that he carries a crook in his hand and often has a dinner-bag slung round his back. The crook and dinner-bag outfit may have helped to spread the prevailing idea that he leads an easy, lazy life, because he only attracts attention when out with his sheep. Few people know the extent of his daily duties according to the seasons, and very few have an opportunity to examine all the articles he uses for his work.

A shepherd's possessions are generally divided between his home and his hut on the farm. At home is his "shepherd's box," which contains personal treasures. Some drawer usually holds his favourite sheep-shears in a pouch, ready for use. Sticks suitable for crook handles are laid out on a rack to dry and season, and if there be a shed in his garden many tools and interesting things will surely be found there.

Shepherds' huts on wheels are sometimes good wooden structures. These can be made into comfortable temporary homes at lambing time, and are appreciated far more than farmers may guess. Unfortunately we often notice the cheaper ugly ones of painted iron, which spoil the landscape, but this is not by the wish of the shepherds, who find them draughty and uncomfortable and unfit for anything but rough storage. Whichever kind it may be it is always a home for a lot of oddments. In addition to articles included in shepherds' gear there is generally a box of tins and bottles containing medicines and mixtures for various purposes—a poor lot of rubbish to the casual observer, but very valuable to their owner when occasion arises. Sacks of food are frequently stored on the floor and one corner usually holds odd tools, such as the broom, prong, turnip pecker, and a pair or two of "sheep-bows."

The charm of a hut is that one never knows what may be hiding in it—an old blue umbrella, perhaps, a bell or two, or an old crook. A small curio, a "shepherds' crown," or fossil, may rest on a ledge, a "dirt-knocker," or other interesting thing may hide among the bits of wood, wire, and other trifles that always seem to find their way into the hut. Occasionally a bunch of rabbit wires on a nail or a well-used gun tell their own tale. Various other possessions are given a temporary home in the hut according to the work on hand. The door is therefore padlocked, and the shepherd either carries the key or hides it near the hut.

At lambing time, visitors who have the privilege of inspecting one of the big wooden huts with a chimney, that is used as a lodging, may find one part arranged as a sleeping bunk. By the door one corner is occupied by a small stove, with kettle, milk saucepan and firewood; the other by broom and crook. Somewhere there will be crocks for meal-times, a feeding bottle for lambs, and other receptacles, whose mysterious contents, so useful in the lambing-fold, do not always agree with the labels that still adhere to them. The lantern is an important item: in the daytime it hangs on its nail, but at night it stands ready for instant use. More often than not it is a modern one, but here and there may be discovered a horn lantern of the old type still doing duty, treasured by a shepherd who understands its value.

The casual mention of these few things leads to consideration of all the rest. A full list of shepherd's gear includes many items, and the following notes record

# THE SHEPHERD'S POSSESSIONS

those in use at this date. In most cases they are the property of the shepherd.

In continuation of previous paragraphs it seems convenient to refer first to those items which are in use at lambing time. Crook and lantern are referred to in special chapters, and the broom used for sweeping out the hut needs no description. The prong is in constant use among straw and hay, and is also used for transferring the mangolds from the heap. These are either taken to the pens in a wheelbarrow or carried from the heap in a large wooden trug-basket. Where sufficient material for a well-made thatched fold is allowed by the farmer a thatching needle is used. It may be a home-made wooden one—a stick whittled down to a flat point at one end with an eye burned through it—or it may be an iron needle, either one with a handle or one of the very old ones—a thin iron rod with an eye in the pointed end.

In cases where a ewe does not give sufficient milk for her lambs, or if one is not getting sufficient, or where an orphan is waiting for a foster-mother, the shepherd has an extra duty. The babies must have a regular supply of warm milk, hence the necessity for a saucepan in his outfit at lambing time. The lambs' feeding bottle is of interest. Often it is an ordinary wine or spirit bottle fitted with a rubber teat, but in some cases the teat is made in the old-fashioned way, of a piece of elder twig with the pith removed, bound round with rag. Another variety was made by converting a small new oil can into a feeder. This was done at the local forge. The little neck of the can was transferred to the shoulder for a filler, and stoppered with a cork, while the neck hole was plugged with an elder teat bound with rag. This type was considered by some to be more handy and durable than a glass bottle. A specimen, formerly used at Washington, is to be seen in Worthing Museum.

The pitching-iron (also known as the " iron bar " or " fold bar ") is a very important item in every shepherd's outfit. It is a thick round rod, to which a heavy tapering point has been added by a blacksmith. When pitching a fold, the tool is used to make holes for the stakes and to drive the stakes deep in the ground. It is in daily use, and consequently an " iron " that is comfortable to handle becomes a favourite tool.

Sheep bows (sometimes called " blue bows," and " strods ") are made from natural branches of forked shape (like the letter Y in wood) shaved down to the required size. The long end is pointed, and each of the " arms " is bored, near the top, with two or three holes. An iron rod, attached to the bows by chain and staple, is used to connect any pair of holes. Bows are made for holding the heads of sheep and lambs while they are being tidied for the market or sheep fair. The pointed end of the Y is driven into the ground and the head of an animal is securely held in the fork by the little iron rod. By this means the shepherd's hands are left free to use his stiff brush and sharp shears to advantage.

The brush and shears are mentioned above. The sharpening stone accompanies the shears, but the carrier or shears pouch is a link with the past. Pouches were made to hold three or four pairs of shears. They consist of strong sheaths of leather joined together, all the ends being covered by one stout leather cap. A short strap sewn on the back sheath was passed between the shears and fastened by a buckle on the front of the pouch. This kept the shears in their place as they were carried upside down. A long strap attached enabled the shepherd or shearer to sling the lot round him as one carries a satchel. Some of these old black pouches, handed down from one generation to another, are treasured possessions, and are in excellent condition, although made so long ago. I have one with the date 1826 pricked in the leather.

The fact that shears were greased and pouches oiled when not in use accounts for the good preservation of these interesting specimens of old leather work.

Trimming time is followed by the use of a marking iron (the farmer's property) and the shepherd's paint-pot. Rams are marked with numbers, and many shepherds own a set of numbering irons. These are used like a marking iron, as described in the interview with Walter Wooler, while for marking in the ears nippers or ear punches must be at hand when required.

There is only occasional use for some items in a shepherd's gear, such as the swaphook and the handbill, the former for cutting lamb creeps through rape and for other purposes, the latter for pointing hurdle stakes and poles and cutting branches to fill gaps in hedges. The turnip pecker is another tool which has a long rest between its useful hours. It has two stout little curved prongs, and is mounted on a strong stiff handle. When sheep are folded on turnips, the roots can be lifted with this tool. Partly eaten roots which might otherwise be trodden in and wasted are hooked out. When root feed is scarce, a careful shepherd's extra work with his pecker benefits both flock and farmer, but the only reward for this tiring addition to so many daily duties is an easy conscience!

The dirt-knocker is not found among the gear of a hill shepherd, but on farms in low-lying localities; where sheep fleeces become matted with winter mud it is very useful. It is a home-made wooden mallet about ten inches or so in length. The mud-laden ends of the fleece are rested on a flat piece of wood or iron held in one hand, and a tap from the little mallet breaks up the unwelcome burden. My specimen came from a Goring shepherd's hut, where three lay in a corner. "I made all they from the same piece of ash," said the shepherd; "it grew not far from here." One of the mallets had a thick square, tapering handle. "That one isn't as I made it," he remarked; "I had a man to help, an' he diddun' like *he*, so he changed his handle, an' now *I* don't like using *he!*"

Tailing irons are little spade-shaped irons (with wedge-shaped section) on rods with handles of wood or a plain ring of iron. With these lambs' tails are docked, the red-hot iron severing and cauterising at the same time. The skin of the lamb's tail is pulled back before the cut is made, so that, when released, it helps to cover the wound. Tailing is necessary to ensure cleanliness. In some places a knife takes the place of tailing irons. On one farm at Sompting it was found that for some unknown reason tails did not heal well until a change was made and a knife used. This fact leads to further consideration of the shepherd's knife, the use of which I have already described as follows :

> "Few people would think of the shepherd's big clasp-knife as an important tool, but it is in fact one of the most essential items in his outfit. Among its many uses I have seen it take the place of a surgeon's lancet at lambing time. With it the shepherd cuts and trims sticks of all kinds, including crook sticks; cuts out strap tackle, yokes and pegs, pares the hooves of sheep, and cuts up his lunch; while during any day a dozen other odd things may provide other uses for it. The shepherd has to rely on his own efforts to such an extent that without a strong, sharp knife very little could be done."[1]

The ruddle-pot, though only used at pairing time, is an important item to the shepherd. Rams are freely coloured with the ruddle, or red chalk, and the transfer

[1] *Downland Treasure*, by Barclay Wills, reprinted by permission of the publishers, Messrs. Methuen and Co., Ltd.

*Photo by the Author*

"CANNISTER" BELL

BELLS MOUNTED ON CHIN-BOARDS

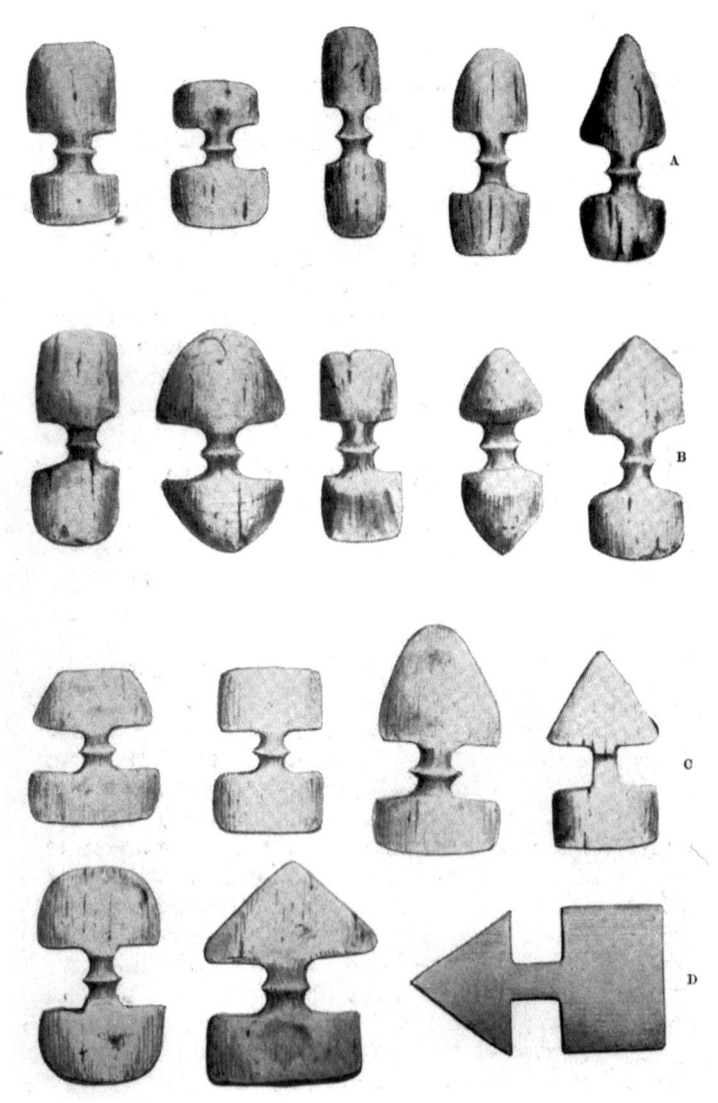

**LOCKYERS**
A and B made of Yew Wood.
C and D made of Bone.
(*From a sketch by the Author*)

of the colour to the ewes tells the shepherd what he must know ere he can count the days on the calendar and arrange for the preparation of his lambing fold at the correct date.

The fly-powder tin is one of a crowd of oddments and may be regarded as representing all the range of mysterious pots, tins and bottles which comprise the " medicine cupboard " of the shepherd.

Two other items complete the ordinary list of shepherd's gear—the umbrella (described in a separate chapter) and the bag which the shepherd carries to and fro each day. It is of no set pattern—simply a bag or satchel to contain his dinner, a tea bottle, and any small thing which may be required. It is usually slung over the shoulder by a strap held in the hand, or hung over the shoulder on the crook. I have seen various quaint things come out of some of these bags at close of day— " shepherds' crowns," ox shoes, flints, rabbits, bells and tackle, wires, split pins and string, and once some flowering bulbs of " Star of Bethlehem " found on the Downs. " Reckon 'tis a pretty flower ! " the shepherd said ; " I be takin' 'em for my garden."

Among some gear at Falmer, belonging to Nelson Coppard, was a dipping hook, once used at sheep washings. As this custom is now almost out of date the hook will soon be regarded as a curio. It was mounted on a stout pole about eight feet long. With it a sheep's head could be ducked under the water or held up as required. Reference is made to the use of the tool in a later chapter on sheep-washing.

On only two occasions I have found a shepherd's stool in use. This is a home-made contrivance—a small piece of strong board with a hole in the centre cut and shaped to receive the end of a short stick. This very useful " extra " to a shepherd's outfit enables the owner to rest for a few minutes while tending when the ground is damp. My specimen is made of oak, and was given to me by Mr. G. Newell whom I met with his flock at Devil's Dyke. He had used it for twenty years. A leather brace end nailed to the underside enabled him to attach it to any convenient button, and he carried the stick separately.

From these notes it will be seen that the average shepherd's gear makes an important list, surprising to those who learn the number of his necessary possessions for the first time. Although many of the articles are quite ordinary, the wooden bows, stool, dirt-knocker, and thatching-needle are of particular interest, for with the carved bell-tackle, described later, they form a series of objects made by the shepherds for their own use.

*Note.*—A picture of Mr. Newell, carrying his stool, appears on another page.

## Shepherds' Umbrellas

To meet a shepherd carrying one of the large old-fashioned umbrellas is already unusual, and such a sight will become worthy of remark by ramblers, for although these useful articles were once part of every shepherd's equipment, they are now out of date.

It is only natural that in course of time each specimen must come to a sudden end through some mishap. Violent gusts of wind, such as we all experience occasionally, have been responsible for the loss of the majority of big umbrellas.

Since war-time it has been almost useless to order one of the old type or to try to get an old frame covered with the original green material. Some modern ones obtained to order for shepherds have proved to be nothing more than an " out size " of the ordinary black-covered umbrella, and have provoked hearty curses from those who parted with a fair sum and sent cash with order, in the hope that they would obtain what they required.

Casual mention of big umbrellas to any old shepherd will usually draw some reply in praise of them. Even those who have a well-worn specimen and do not carry it for fear of being considered "too old-fashioned" by employer and others are willing to admit that, like the old round frocks, "there is nothing to compare with them." A shepherd provided with one, and clad in his thick overcoat, had only to push his way, backwards, into a bush, crouch down and hold the big umbrella over him, and he was protected from the heaviest rain. It was usual to carry one to and fro in stormy weather, and although big and cumbersome, they were easily managed by attaching a cord to the handle and the ferrule end. The cord, adjusted to the proper length, was put over the head and under one arm so that the umbrella was slung across the shepherd's back. I have an old specimen which measures four feet across when opened and which weighs three pounds, yet, carried in this way, its size is scarcely noticed.

Some umbrellas had ribs of cane and some of whalebone. Many frames of the latter kind, when done with, have found their way to some dealer's store, where a good price is asked for the whalebone ribs.

When interviewing Michael Blann I spoke of big umbrellas; and he said: "Once I had one with me when I walked miles home from Lewes in a storm of rain and wind. A gust got under it and blew it to bits, so I threw it in the ditch. Afterwards I bought another one and was caught in another storm. I was on top of a bank. The wind came very suddenly and lifted the umbrella and me with it and dropped us down under none the worse. That was a storm, and no mistake! Another gust came and blew the umbrella nearly inside out, and as I turned to face the wind it blew back to its proper shape again, but before I had time to think much of these wonderful antics a still more violent wind shattered him altogether."

Many somewhat similar incidents are remembered by other old shepherds, but the most entertaining one I have heard was recorded in my *Bypaths in Downland* and is reprinted here :

"One day I was making inquiries from a shepherd regarding these big umbrellas, and he related how he once got some fun out of the use of 'the big 'un.' The flocks of three adjoining farms were each in the charge of a young shepherd, and he was one of the three. They would sometimes meet at one particular spot for a chat, and on one occasion were caught in a sudden heavy shower. Not far from where they stood a man and a maid were sitting on a bank, and one of the shepherds suggested that my friend should take his big umbrella and share it with the couple. On the spur of the moment he accepted the challenge and walked across to them with the big umbrella open. To his amazement the girl's companion rose and ran away as fast as he could, leaving her on the bank. He evidently suspected from the young shepherd's advance and the merriment of the others that some plot was afoot, and, like the coward he was, left the girl to her fate. It would seem that he had no particular claim to her affection and that she was inclined to appreciate the young shepherd's action, for she sat quite still and allowed him to shelter her from the rain in gallant fashion. 'I diddun' mine they cheps grinnin',' he told me, 'fur she wur a purty gel, an' tarked to I. "Doan't 'ee putt t' umbereller down," she says, when t' rain stopped; "kip 'un up a bit, fur I likes bein' 'ere 'long o' you." But I *did* putt 'un down, fur t' dog telled I to.' The old shepherd chuckled and rubbed his head. 'Damme, I'd nigh forgot 'bout it all,' he said, 'till you comed tarkin' 'bout they umberellers!'"[1]

### BY THE WAY

Green is the track that climbs the hill
From this old farm in hollow still;
Wind in the west; across the sky
Big black clouds are hurrying by;
Two little boys, with roguish smile,
Standing beside the well-worn stile;
Four merry eyes, so good to see!—
" Mischiful trimmers they two boys be "
Said one of the farmer's men. " I know
Whenever I sees 'em a-grinnin' so,
They've jus' done *summat*, an' runned away!—
We'll mek 'em tell us t' joke to-day!"

. . . . .

" Faather's jus' gon' over t' brow—
He be shepherd—he said, jus' now,
T' way t' rooks be flyin' 'bout
Reckoned he wouldn' goo fur widout
His ol' umbrellar—he sent us back
To bring 'un along, so me an' Jack
Went into t' shed—we got 'un untied
An' dropped some han'fuls o' bran inside!
We hurried an' ran up hill again
An' now we're wait'n for it to rain—
Ef doos I reckon he'll look for we
D'rectly he comes back home to tea!"

B. W.

### Horn Lanterns

The peculiar fascination which clings to objects connected with past days has already extended to the old horn lanterns which were commonly used by Sussex shepherds at lambing time.

[1] Reprinted by permission of the publishers, Messrs. Methuen and Co., Ltd.

As I look back on all the hours spent in the company of shepherds, under all sorts of conditions, I cannot recall a more fascinating sight than a certain shepherd, while on his round in a lambing fold at night, carrying a horn-windowed candle-lantern. Until I stood there, a silent watcher in the shadow, and experienced those moments of pure delight, I had not realized that any artificial light could hold such charm. At first I had carried the lantern myself, stepping softly among the resting ewes, and holding it while the shepherd performed the necessary services, but later I stood back while he went round alone, simply for the pleasure of gazing at the scene. The cloaked figure with the lantern seemed to glide among the sheep; the pale, mellow light flickered over his garments, over recumbent forms in the straw, and over the hurdle-pens; then, as the lantern was set down by his feet, like a great glow-worm, the yellow rays lit up the shepherd's features, and shone upon a newly born baby.

As my friend returned to the hut I drew further back, to see him ascend the steps. The door opened; the lighted interior swallowed up the lantern's rays, and the big figure was silhouetted for a moment in the doorway. He looked round for me. "Oh, there you be, then," he said, as I followed him in, amused that I should have been watching him at his work. Little he knew of the beauty I had found in the homely scene transformed by the magic of lantern-light!

With the possession of a fine horn lantern, used by shepherd Jesse Moulding of Goring, my interest increased. Variation in size and design of other specimens suggested that more might be learned about them. From the oldest country shops where they were once sold I was referred to wholesale dealers, who, in turn, introduced me to the actual makers. Messrs. Walker & Loach of Birmingham, who specialized in the manufacture of these lanterns, kindly furnished me with some details about them, and sent me an old price list from which I note that horn lanterns were once made in eight sizes, as follows :

|  | Height at Shoulder | Diameter |
|---|---|---|
| No. 1 | 6 in. | $4\frac{1}{2}$ in. |
| 2 | $6\frac{1}{2}$ ,, | 5 ,, |
| 3 | 7 ,, | $5\frac{1}{2}$ ,, |
| 4 | 8 ,, | 6 ,, |
| 5 | $8\frac{1}{2}$ ,, | $6\frac{1}{2}$ ,, |
| 6 | $9\frac{1}{4}$ ,, | $7\frac{1}{4}$ ,, |
| 7 | 10 ,, | 8 ,, |
| 8 | 12 ,, | $8\frac{3}{4}$ ,, |

Two types of lantern were made. The one termed " Plain " has the crown pierced by three sets of holes—one large, surrounded by six small, in each set. (This type, if lighted indoors, throws a pretty pattern of twenty-one spots of light on the ceiling.) The other type, termed " Dormered," has the holes hidden by three little covers like dormer windows, each pierced with an opening in the shape of a cross or with many small holes.

The horn windows were fitted with wire guards except in lanterns of small size.

Messrs Walker & Loach wrote to me as follows :

" Our firm, in the past, specialized in the manufacture of the horn lantern, and we have made many hundreds of grosses. Unfortunately, for some years now, the horn leaf has not been obtainable, and this has caused the trade to become obsolete.

" We still make up a lantern which we term a Horn Lantern, fitted up with panes which are a substitute for the old horn leaf. They are nothing like as good, and we look upon it as a dying trade.

"The firm we procured the horn leaf from was Mr. John Harmer, 68 Pope Street, Birmingham. We understand these people procured the leaf in the rough from a firm at Bewdley, near Kidderminster, and afterwards dried and polished it to the small sample we send you herewith. They gave up business about December, 1915."

The two usual types of lantern are figured here. In addition to these I was shown the remains of a very old one, used on a Sompting farm, in which the windows were divided by a tin strip and held two small pieces of horn instead of the usual single sheet.

The safety which results from the use of a horn lantern in a straw-littered lambing fold accounted for the old shepherds' strong preference for them. A chance knock or a kick from a ewe may have split a horn leaf sometimes, but no dreadful consequences followed. The interview with Michael Blann records an actual instance of the danger of an oil lamp used under similar conditions.

As the last stocks in country shops sold out it became difficult for some shepherds to obtain a horn lantern, and the use of glass-windowed candle-lanterns followed. A fine heavy specimen was used by a shepherd—the late John Norris, of Coate Farm, Durrington—about sixty years ago. It may be seen in Worthing Museum.

The use of modern sheets of flexible transparent composition has made it possible for anyone to acquire a lantern of the old type, for the metal part is still made to the same old pattern; but it is good to own a real horn one that was once used by a shepherd, for some subtle charm still clings to it.

We may try its effect in place of our usual indoor light when we have time to rest and day-dream. As shadows deepen, the pale rays from the candle seem to show brighter through the horn, and as the same soft glow that shone on the hurdle pens and sheep with newly born babies illuminates the room, half-forgotten scenes of folds, and shepherds, and small tottering lambs return to us. In fancy we hear once more the clamour as mothers and children call to one another. Other pictures follow, and we live past hours over again, for there is memory-magic in the light from the old horn lantern!

### Shepherds' Clothes

When asked about clothes worn in past days a shepherd remarked to me: " To write about round-frocks and corduroys and things is quite right, but I don't think you ought to put it down that every shepherd wore this or that—sometimes he did, *if he could get it!* If he couldn't, then he had to do with what he had. Shepherds' wages were very low; why, when I was saving to be married, and buying bits of furniture, I wore *anything*. For a long time I wore an old frock-coat. I didn't care what I looked like, for it saved me from spending more money. If you had an old photo of me taken at that time you might think shepherds wore frock-coats—and you would be wrong!"

This point of view was confirmed by another man whom I interviewed. He said: " When I left home, over sixty years ago, I walked miles to get to Brighton, to save my bit of money. There was some delay before I got work and I had to sell my dog to get enough to keep me till I started. My wages were eleven shillings a week and I wore out my clothes faster than I could buy new ones. I wore anything I could get, and it was pretty rough sometimes on the hills without very much clothing!"

Many shepherds of to-day, although receiving better wages, are still obliged to wear what they can get instead of what they would choose. It does not seem possible to obtain the old types of hard-wearing materials in suits or overcoats at ordinary prices : the corduroy has no lasting quality; the overcoats will not stand a day's rain. The consequence is that the modern shepherd is generally badly dressed in a poor corduroy or a shoddy suit, and old overcoats of shoddy material or ugly khaki army coats have taken the place of the big fleecy coats and the second-hand cavalry cloaks which were worn by some old men and which gave them such an imposing and picturesque appearance.

Old leather leggings are still seen, for they were frequently handed down or passed on from one shepherd to another. Strong boots and leggings are important items in every shepherd's outfit. The short leggings— so useful on a dewy morning—are sometimes removed at the fold if the moisture dries off, and are carried home at night. In the picture of Tom Rusbridge an interesting item still worn by some shepherds is seen: "false tongues" or large pieces of thick leather which are tied over the laced fronts of boots to keep out the dew and rain. Mr. Rusbridge offered to make me a pair as specimens, and was amused to know that I preferred to have the actual ones he wore, which are shown in the photo.

One small point is worth notice in connection with shepherds' dress : the fact that when at work the men usually have the neck and throat bare and free to the air.

In the chapter on Michael Blann there is a reference to hats of such tough material that they would support a man's weight. Subsequently a chance question on the subject brought a caustic comment from a younger man. " You mustn't believe all these ol' fellers tell you," he said, " some of 'em can mek up a good yarn if they get anybody to listen ! " But proof was waiting for me in *Sussex Folk and Sussex Ways*, by the Rev. John Coker Egerton, Rector of Burwash, who died in 1888, aged fifty-eight. The following account of home-made linens and of a village hatter who made these excellent hats is taken from that book :

"Within the recollection of many persons still alive we grew flax, bleached it, carded it, spun and wove it at home. In many of our cottages there are yet to be found sheets, tablecloths, and other articles of linen which seems to defy the power of time. Doubtless they are now kept more as curiosities than for use; still they have borne an amount of wear and tear which is certainly not expected of more modern goods.

"We had our own hatter within my own memory, though when I knew him he had ceased to work at his trade. His productions had the character of being everlasting. It was said to be simply impossible to wear them out. One particular kind of hat, called 'dog's-hair' hats, had this further peculiarity, that if a man wished to reach something, say from a shelf, and found himself hardly tall enough, he had nothing to do but to put down his hat upon the ground and stand upon it; it would bear him without a sign of yielding. A man who used to wear one of these imperishable helmets told me that till it got well sweated to the shape of the head, wearing it was 'all one as if you had your head in the stocks.' The two finer kinds of material used in our hats were 'hare's flick' or 'rabbit flick.' Hats of the former kind were, I believe, expensive and quite aristocratic, and were reserved principally for Sundays and special occasions."

Shepherd Tom Rusbridge told me that, when he was young, shepherds and farmers wore hard felt hats with flat crowns. The shepherds painted theirs, mostly grey, and when they were done they were shiny and would keep out any wet. Dick Flint, a Findon shepherd, referred to these as "half-high" hats.

The last time I saw shepherd Frank Upton he was wearing a stout old white smock, which had been shortened and opened down the front for convenience. I spoke of slaty-grey ones and found that he used to wear them years ago. "Smocks are nearly gone out," he said, "but at one time all us shepherds wore them and when we went to Lewes Fair on the 21st September we used to make it Clothing Day as well as Fair Day. We always went to Browne and Crosskey's shop for smocks and gaiters and long gaiters and big overcoats and anything we wanted."

A visit to Mr. E. A. Wheatley, the proprietor of Browne and Crosskey, of High Street, Lewes, confirmed these facts. Mr. Wheatley has been connected with the business for nearly forty years, and his father entered the firm in 1860. I was pleased to find that photographs of some of the old shepherds, which I was carrying, were at once recognized as those of customers.

Mr. Wheatley produced various items for my inspection: first some old documents relating to the firm, which although not connected with shepherds, were very interesting; then patterns of the drab and slate-grey linen of which Sussex round-frocks were made. A finished smock of each colour was shown to me; also a roll of the drab linen used for the purpose. The smocks were of the usual type, with excellent "smocking," but without elaborate ornament.

Orders for smocks are still received occasionally, but not from shepherds. The last sold were for the use of beaters at shooting parties. Our chat about the subject reminded Mr. Wheatley of a quaint incident which provided a new name for them. A countryman once entered the store and said: "I want a 'og stopper!" He explained that when working among pigs, and he

# THE SHEPHERD'S POSSESSIONS

found it necessary to stop one, he got in its way and sat on his heels. The pig could not dodge between his legs, for the round frock effectually stopped its rush!

The outfitting department was at one time at the top of a staircase, and when shepherds arrived on 21st September they would often leave their big coats and crooks and dogs at the foot of the stairs while they bought the big overcoats and smocks and what else they required. The 21st of September was a busy day, and it was the custom to put packing-cases on the path outside the shop to serve as seats for wives and friends waiting for the customers.

A query about shepherds' umbrellas resulted in further interest. The firm supplied these too. I was shown a stock of modern ones of all sizes, but all had steel frames and black covers. Mr. Wheatley said the old covers were green and that those still in use have faded to the familiar bluish shade. Many of these umbrellas were very large and it was not unusual for a man to say: "I want a new tent."

The long tan leather gaiters are not stocked now. At one time it was usual for the actual maker of them to call in the summer and take orders for supplies of gaiters for winter trade. He still makes them to order if required.

The old days are gone, but the old shepherds are remembered at the shop, just as the shop is remembered by the shepherds, and I was glad that a chance remark heard on the hills led me to Lewes to prove that it is so.

# SHEEP-CROOKS AND SHEEP-BELLS

### Sheep-crooks

AMONG all the shepherd's possessions, apart from his dog, his sheep-crook takes first place. It is his constant companion. With it he catches sheep by the hind-leg, and young lambs by the neck. Without it he would be unable to do the work he does.

Sometimes a " best " crook is kept at home, and only used on special occasions, but the one in daily use must suit his particular fancy, otherwise it will be superseded at the first opportunity. Not every shepherd we meet is thoroughly satisfied with the crook he is using—it may be a little too light or a little too heavy, or too long in the guide, or too large in the head for his sheep. There are so few good crook-makers about now that it is not always an easy matter to get a crook which satisfies all requirements. Just as a rambler may prefer one old stick, or a workman one favourite tool, so a shepherd likes a crook which is comfortable to handle, and should he acquire one, by chance, which is satisfactory, in all respects he will not be persuaded to part with it easily or change it for another. (The interview with Jack Cox records an instance of the reliability of a crook to the use of which its owner has grown accustomed.)

It is a surprise to those who make even a casual study of crooks to find what variety there is to note and what detail there is to discover. The very old ones of wrought iron are often well made, but those fashioned from pieces of gun barrels are undoubtedly the best. So many different and quaintly designed crooks of wrought iron have been produced by local blacksmiths in Sussex that a book would be needed to record them all. I have even seen one made from a golf club. It came from the smithy on Saddlescombe Farm. I have an old iron crook, last used at Goring, which has the barrel edged with saw-like teeth. Possibly this was made by someone who considered that a better grip on the stick would be obtained in this way. Enquiries proved that crooks with toothed barrels are considered to be uncommon. I have another quaint specimen from Albourne (probably made for use among lambs or very small sheep) which has a tiny head and a very short guide with a big curl.

A limited number of *brass* crooks were once made at Brighton. They were produced secretly at the railway workshop. The first one, made as a curio, resulted in requests for more, but many of those who acquired them found them liable to snap asunder during use. Very few specimens are to be found now, and those I have traced are kept as curios by their owners. My discovery of the first brass crook made is related in the interview with Charles Trigwell, and a picture of the crook accompanies this chapter.

In studying crooks one gradually learns to find the greatest delight in the best work. Specimens made from gun barrels are so beautiful and attractive when thoroughly clean that the majority of wrought iron ones appear rough and clumsy beside them.

The best crooks are doubtless the result of long trials of various designs by different makers. The preference for certain well-known patterns, such as the *old* Pyecombe, the Kingston, and the Falmer ones, merely shows that these won the approval of those who used them.

Little differences, such as weight, the outline of the

head, or the space between the guide and the barrel, are often arranged to suit individual tastes. The utility of a crook is always the chief point for consideration. The only part of a crook where any tendency to ornament is found is in the " guide," which is the long thin end bent at an angle to the barrel and which usually has the tip curled round to avoid a sharp point. The guide slides round a sheep's leg and no harm is done. The crook is raised as it catches hold and the sheep's leg is lifted. This allows the shepherd to seize the sheep and do what may be necessary.

Occasionally a crook may be found in which the long thin tail is curled round three or four times, merely for ornament. I have known a " tail " closed in the ordinary way to be opened so that the curl could be cleaned and polished with emery to match the rest of the crook, which was as bright as clean silver. It is rather unusual to find one kept so bright—they are mostly dulled by very slight rust. One shepherd told me that he considered a bright crook unsafe in thunderstorms on the hills and would not hold one at such times.

The beautiful workmanship found in some crooks was doubtless responsible for the incorrect idea that they are merely ornamental handles for staves, yet, as I wrote in one of my books, it is easy to understand how such an idea originated. A shepherd often uses his crook as a staff until the need to use it for its legitimate purpose arises, but a moment later the handle may become a staff once again. I have seen a hedger at Falmer going home, and using his long-handled hedge bill as a staff, yet this tool could not be mistaken for anything but a tool— it was merely carried that way for convenience. So with the sheep-crook. Sometimes the barrel, in a line with the stick, certainly offers a convenient grip for the hand, but when the stick is a long one (say five feet or so) and the shepherd is short, his hand seldom touches the

A SHEARING GANG AT SADDLESCOMBE FARM, ABOUT 1888

**FRANK SHEPHERD
THE TAR-BOY**
*(Enlarged from the photo of
the shearing gang by Mr. Eric
Heard of Hove)*

**HORN LANTERNS**
*(Photo by the Author)*

metal. No argument, however ingenious, can prove the point suggested, because the crook is a *tool* for a specific purpose and is fitted with a new *handle* as often as required.

Although many smiths must have been noted for crook-making about their own districts, a certain number gained a very wide reputation. Among these were three who made crooks of distinctive design at Falmer, Kingston-by-Lewes, and Pyecombe. Shepherds sometimes refer to their crooks as " hooks," but the term is now more often used in connection with old specimens made at Pyecombe forge than those made elsewhere.

One of the old makers of crooks at Pyecombe forge, named Berry, became famous for his " Pyecombe hooks." An authentic example is figured here. As noted in a former book, it belonged to Mr. Frank Upton, shepherd at Brown's Farm, West Blatchington, and was last used by him about 1916. It was made by Berry for Mr. Upton's father. Although there is no record of the actual date, Mr. Upton stated that as it was before he was born it must have been some time previous to 1864. From a rough estimate of the duration of tenancies since Berry's time it would appear that the last of his crooks were made about 1855 or before. The last tenant of the forge, Mr. Charles Mitchell, has been making crooks there for nearly sixty years, so that some of his earlier examples, such as the one used by Mr. Walter Wooler of Pyecombe, have already become specimens to be treated with that respect which is due to the oldest examples of one of the Sussex crafts ; but the crook figured here is one of that famous pattern which brought renown to Pyecombe forge that has lasted until to-day.

" Kingston " crooks were made by Philip Hoather, the blacksmith of Kingston-by-Lewes, who worked at his forge for fifty-seven years. He made excellent crooks, and many shepherds preferred a "Kingston" to any other kind. The one illustrated here was a good sample of his work and had been in use for twenty-five years when Nelson Coppard gave it to me. Like the Pyecombe specimen, its design is good and it is well balanced. Too much weight in the guide is enough to make a perceptible difference in the swing of the tool when a sheep is being caught, unless the handle is gripped very firmly—a point that is only appreciated fully by a shepherd or by a smith who understands the use of a crook.

"Falmer" crooks were made by a blacksmith named Green who was manager at Falmer forge. A distinctive feature of his crooks was the beautifully curled end of the guide. This was not made on the point of the anvil, but produced by using a little home-made iron tool which was fixed in a vice. The outline of each crook was made to a pattern scratched on a slate.

From a chat with Mr. Starks, who once worked under Green, I gathered that these crooks were really bargains at the prices paid for them. Green's delight in this special work and his anxiety for perfection in finish resulted in beautiful work, but his assistants did not share in his pride. The forge was a very unrestful place while such work was in progress, and Mr. Starks has never found enjoyment in crook-making since those days. It is probable that if the hours spent on crooks had been charged up properly to each job the total would have been far more than the prices received from the shepherds who bought them.

The handle for the crook, known as the "crook-stick," is an important item. A good, strong, straight one is preferred. Hazel seems to be the favourite in Sussex, but ground-ash is often used, and occasionally a straight holly, cherry, or other stick is seen. Most shepherds endeavour to store up and season a few spare sticks. I have seen a live ground ash which had been bent down flat and tightly pegged, when young, by a shepherd for future use. He showed it to me and cut it off while I waited with him.

Worn and weakened crook-sticks are replaced with new ones if possible, for if a stick snaps off short owing to age it is necessary to put the barrel of the crook in a fire to burn out the stick end. This is the reason why many old iron crooks are much worn in the barrel or have had that part shortened or repaired. A shepherd who treasures his crook would rather replace the stick occasionally than fire the barrel. To get a crook off its handle it is struck smartly inside the curved head with a heavy rod, or a poker, or anything suitable, and it drops off suddenly. To fit a new stick in the barrel is not so easy as one would think. To do so correctly the stick is carefully whittled to fit the barrel and put in lightly. The shepherd then tests it by resting the stick across his half-closed hand while his arm hangs by his side. The guide of the crook should point upward. If it topples to one side, it must be fitted on the stick again, otherwise the tool would feel top-heavy or difficult to manage. Directly the stick rides perfectly on the hand one is aware of the change, and a few smart taps on the ground with the end of the stick secures the crook in its place.

I have a crook-stick (from Nelson Coppard) which was used as a tally-stick for noting the measurement of wire required. Fourteen notches are cut in it. Another notch, twenty-five inches from the end, records the length of a snake which he killed with the crook.

Certain vague references in print suggest that at one time it was customary in some parts for shepherds to sit and carve their crook-sticks, but in spite of careful inquiry I have been unable to trace any actual instance among Sussex shepherds. If it ever was customary in the county and the custom died out, the absence of evidence is probably accounted for by the comparatively short life of a crook-stick, whereas old wooden bell-yokes, made by shepherds, and often referred to as "*wooden crooks*," were carefully finished and sometimes carved with numbers, initials, dates, and designs.

There is only one way to appreciate the many little details relating to the designs and uses of crooks, and that is to learn them from the actual makers and users; not from one man, but from many, and to handle such specimens of smiths' work.

### STORY OF SHEPHERD M

This is a tale of Shepherd M,
As it was told to me;
He only knew his native hills
Though he was eighty-three;
The counties round were " furrin parts ";
He never had been far
Until his grandchild wed a man
Who owned a motor car.

When first they brought the car along
To take him for a spin
'Twas not as easy as they thought
To get the old man in;
He asked for time to " tidy up,"
And made the couple look
In great surprise when he appeared
With gaiters, smock and crook.

In vain they both explained to him
That smocks were " out of date " !
In vain they bade him hurry and
Declared they would be late !
Old Granfer would not budge; he stood
With frown upon his brow—
" I've allus wored dis smock," he said,
" An' I be ready now ! "

"Come on then," said the eager pair,
"But put the *crook* away—
You won't want *that!*" The old man's face
At once expressed dismay!
"What! goo outdoors widout de crook!—
Why, I'd be reg'lar froughten!
I ne'er bin out widout un yet,
An' I *wunt* goo widout un!"

And so at last they started off
The "furrin parts" to see;
They showed him all the country round
And finished up at B——
They took him to a tea-shop smart—
It made the people stare
To see a quaint old shepherd with
A smock and crook in there.

He stared about at everything
With wondering, child-like gaze,
For everyone, to his idea,
Had most unusual ways.
I heard of many things he said
On that eventful day,
But, of them all, I should have liked
To hear the old man say:
"What! goo outdoors widout de crook!—
Why! I'd be reg'lar froughten!
I ne'er bin out widout un yet,
An' I *wunt* goo widout un!"

B. W.


### Sheep-Bells

How restful it is to recline on Downland turf when sunbeams chase cloud-shadows across valley and hill, and robe the rampion flowers in a purer blue! How restful, then, to listen idly to the music from bells on the sheep that gradually approach and surround us, and as gradually wander away!

How restful to the town-tired brain is this bell music, even in winter, when we tramp over the hills and listen to the notes ringing out sharply in the frosty air! Then we hear the bells as the shepherd likes to hear them. He notes the carrying power of each one, and enjoys the music. As we slacken our pace after a tramp and the light changes and warns us that the afternoon is passing, it may be our fortune to hear the wafted sound of bells telling of the return of a flock to the fold. Ting, ting, ting; ting-tang; ting-tong! Faster they go! how eagerly the sheep hurry home! The big wattle-edged fold, where food awaits them, is "home" to them! Every bell sounds in that last rush. We may hear various notes as they scamper through the "door," from canisters, perhaps, or clucks and other iron bells, from cup or latten bells—they may all be picked out by their songs. Chiming effects are now over for the day. Intermittent half-muffled notes whisper to the shepherd as he "tidies up" before leaving his "family" for the night, and presently they cease, one by one, as the sheep sink down to rest.

Sheep-bell music does not seem out of place in the open air; it does not disturb the peace of the countryside as does the sound of an instrument played there. The jingle may be incessant at times, but it does not fidget us as a tune would do if constantly repeated. Unconsciously we note the simple chords when two or three bells ring together. Almost unconsciously we realize that the ancient Downland, the immemorial custom of tending flocks, and the songs of old bells all blend together in some subtle way and cause us to respond to the music. It is this feeling of appreciation which is one of the chief reasons for a shepherd's delight in his bells. Apart from the well-known habit of putting bells on the leaders of a flock or on those inclined to wander, a shepherd will often reserve favourite bells for some sheep that show, by the motion of their heads when feeding, that they will "make a good rattle" when fitted with the treasured specimens. The words "a good rattle" or "a tidy rattle" are used by some shepherds when commenting on bells.

The following paragraph, reprinted from *Bypaths in Downland*, sums up the reasons for the use of sheep-bells in Sussex:

"There is no doubt whatever that bells do serve a useful purpose at times by informing a shepherd as to the whereabouts of his flock from a distance. This is especially the case when the sheep are on the hills where mists are prevalent at certain times. To stand with a shepherd on the Downs and hear the bells chiming when mist blots out the landscape is to understand the feeling which prompts him to arrange for the music. Even in ordinary clear weather the advantage of bells on the leaders of a flock or those inclined to stray is readily noticed. Many farms include a tract of Downland brow and bottom, often studded over with furze bushes, and the shepherd is enabled to locate his team without unnecessary climbing. I have also known instances when the sudden rattle of bells at night has warned the shepherd of the visit of two-legged or four-legged intruders. In addition to the question of usefulness another deciding factor in the use of bells is the shepherd's appreciation of 'bell music.' In some cases this is simply a liking for a useful bell, in others a real pleasure in the actual notes is shown. In the latter case the bells appeal to the shepherd in a special way. They are very sweet company to one who might otherwise notice the extreme quietness in some district. Perhaps you would not suspect how deep is this charm of companionship, which may only find expression in a few words : " They be company, like, to I ! " When you hear this admission you know that the bells have become part of the shepherd's life, and it is easy to understand his loving pride in their possession. Their other uses, already noted, provide an excellent excuse, but the joy of their daily song has really entered into the soul of the man, and outweighs every other consideration.

"It is a fine thing to see old eyes light up at the sound of a favourite bell, when the owner says, softly : 'Hark to 'un, now—*thet* be a good 'un.'"

Although no reference to sheep-bells appears to record the possible or probable date of their introduction into Sussex, the use of them must undoubtedly go back for a considerable period.

In Salisbury I discovered an ancient "saint's hand-bell," and as I cleaned it noted its striking similarity in design, metal, and appearance of surface to some of the very old iron sheep-bells which I had collected on the Sussex Downs. A comparison of them, side by side, suggested that the same method was employed in the construction of both kinds. By a further comparison with other old but unused specimens, I am satisfied that although the ancient hand-bells died out the type lingered on in the form of sheep-bells until less than a hundred years ago.

The Rev. H. T. Ellacombe, in *Bells of the Church*, recorded a process in the manufacture of iron sheep-bells as follows :

" My own opinion is that all these little bells, having the appearance of bronze, were formed in the same way that sheep-bells are made to this day. There is a family at Market Lavington, Wilts, by name of Potter, who have made them for generations. . . . Sheet iron is bent into the form, and riveted together. The intended bell is then bound round with narrow strips of thin brass; some borax is added as a flux, and the whole being enveloped in loam or clay, is submitted to the heat of a furnace, by which the brass is melted and gets intermixed with the heated iron, so rendering it sonorous. Otherwise they were plated with brass, the iron being first dipped in tin, as plated articles of brass are now produced."

Other statements regarding the method of making iron sheep-bells in past days have been published and copied, but according to the opinions of craftsmen who have examined my large series of specimens, the method described by Mr. Ellacombe appeared to them as the most reasonable. Although the record relates to a Wiltshire firm who made "cluck" bells (the favourite type in Wiltshire) the process may be presumed to cover the manufacture of "canisters" and wide-mouthed iron bells. Specimens of each type were among the unused bells, over seventy years old, discovered in Whitechapel Foundry (as described in *Downland Treasure*). Most of these are exhibited in Worthing Museum. They are exactly similar to those still in use on the Sussex Downs, but being unused they are particularly valuable, as they show roughness and unevenness of surface caused by the addition of the brass, which, in used specimens, is worn away in course of years by millions of touches from the wool of the sheep.

Until recent years little interest had been shown in bells—the most fascinating of all the shepherd's possessions. A few people had fallen under their spell, and Dr. P. Habberton Lulham had written of them and shown then in his lectures on Downland subjects; but although they were such a familiar feature of the Downs they were passed over and ignored by many. In 1927 the publication of an appreciative account of the bells and photographs of the various varieties not only created interest in them, but unfortunately put them on a level with other objects regarded as curios. While the fancy lasted the demands of the curio shops resulted in many a deal in old sheep-bells for use as dinner gongs. As is usually the case, dealers forced up prices, consequently, although many nice bells passed through their hands, a large number of rather poor specimens were also passed on at inflated figures. Some rich people who determined to acquire a bell first hand visited shepherds and made them tempting offers; consequently high values still rule in some places where such incidents occurred.

Those who aspire to possess good specimens of every variety now find their hobby rather expensive, but until collections were made by others it was usual for old bells to change hands among shepherds for a shilling each—sometimes even for sixpence each—the explanation being that as the bells were all old they were regarded as second-hand articles.

Bells were once sold at Sussex fairs, particularly at Lewes, and although I have not found a shepherd who actually saw them displayed for sale, the unused specimens from the London foundry referred to above showed precisely how new bells appeared. By looking at them it is easy to reconstruct a scene of a vendor's stock spread out or piled in heaps on the ground for inspection. From the stocks at the fair ground shepherds picked out such bells as they fancied.

For the use of those interested some details relating to the various varieties and details of the home-made tackle for them are included here. The concluding

# SHEEP-CROOKS AND SHEEP-BELLS

paragraphs of the chapter offer the reason for devoting so much space to the subject.

The bells used on sheep on the Sussex Downs are of several types. My list of them is as follows:

*Bells made of sheet iron.*
  Canisters (plain and lacquered)
  Clucks or cluckets
  Wide-mouthed iron bells (three varieties)
  Lewes bells.

*Bells made of brass or bell metal.*
  Wide-mouthed brass bells
  Cup bells (several varieties)
  Horse or " Latten " bells
  White Latten bells
  Crotals or " Rumblers "
  House bells.

In addition to these types several varieties of Swiss cow-bells and other foreign specimens may be found in use to-day, many of them fitted with new (and heavier) tongues. I have noted seven different shapes, and there may be others about.

## Canisters

" Canisters " are the favourite bells in Sussex. Their shape doubtless suggested their name. They are of all sizes—the largest being a little over six inches high—and they vary greatly in proportions, the rarest shape being those with perfectly square crowns. This variation suggests that their size and shape depended solely on the size of the piece of iron sheet available. They were always made with two " staples " on the crown to hold the straps by which they are suspended and those specimens now found with one large staple in the centre of the crown have been repaired and fitted with it to replace the original pair.

The process of manufacture of iron bells (already described) could not give any bell a particular note. This is proved by the fact that in specimens of the same size there is often a great difference in sound. Whereas brass and latten bells of various kinds are cast to exact notes, the old iron bells "knocked up" on an anvil and given tone by the addition of brass or bronze all produced chance notes, irrespective of the size of the bell.

Some canisters give two distinct notes which blend as the tongue swings and strikes the flat side of the bell and then the angle. In such cases the effect is the same as if two bells were in use. These are known to shepherds as "tenor" bells.

Sets of bells known as "rings" were made by selecting those of approximately tuneful notes from a large number. A ring of canisters consisted of eighteen bells—a run of eighteen notes up the scale, sometimes increased to twenty-one or twenty-five. It was not an easy matter to arrange such a long run of bells with more or less approximate notes. By putting a set of twenty-five in order I learned that the method apparently adopted was to make two scales of nine notes, the first bell of one lot starting one note above the first of the others. By this means three bells were duplicated, and when the duplicates were retained they made up the total to twenty-one. Sometimes four "tenor" bells were added—one large and one small to each scale of nine bells. These blended with some of the other bells and increased the "ring" to a total of twenty-five.

Some canister bells were lacquered over with brass, but specimens in good condition are rarely found. I have a specimen from the Lewes district. It is very old, and some of its coat is worn away, but much of its surface is still bright, and quite sufficient to show that those treated in this way must have been very handsome bells.

> I have a row of " canisters "—
> The best that I have found
> In use among the Sussex hills
> As I went tramping round—
> Each from a different shepherd came,
> And each is nearly past
> The point where clever smith's repair
> Would make the favourite last
> A few more years ; but never now
> Will tools, unkind and strong,
> Destroy the marks that prove their age
> Or mar their mellow song !
>
> As flower-gatherers collect
> The finest blooms that grow
> Along the path, and, passing, leave
> The rest behind them, so
> I sought for perfect specimens
> Among each shepherd's hoard ;
> I walked uncounted Downland miles,
> And these are my reward ;
> Each as a portrait is to me,
> For I remember well
> The friendly clasp of every man
> Who owned each precious bell !
>
> B. W.

*Cluckets*

" Cluck " bells or " cluckets " are frequently found on flocks on the Downs, often mingled with canisters. They are a distinct type. There is no flat crown to them as in canisters—merely a ridge, the result of bending the iron sheet.

These bells are the favourite type in Wiltshire, and many have been brought into Sussex by shepherds who crossed the border and settled in this county. Most cluckets are lighter in make than canisters, but occasionally one of exceptionally heavy type is found. Like canisters, cluckets were always fitted with two staples on the crown. The proportion of brass in them is generally less than in canisters, and their notes are more harsh, but as the dull rattling sound "carries" well the bells are popular, especially among those who judge a sheep-bell by its usefulness rather than by its musical effect.

The shape of a cluck bell allows it to be hung close under the sheep's head, instead of dangling, as some bells must do. Its ringing power is thus improved, and the bell is seldom choked with dirt.

*Wide-mouthed Iron Bells*

In addition to canisters and clucks there is a type of bell still in use without any particular name. I refer to it as the "wide-mouthed iron bell." Whereas clucks have the crown wider than the mouth (see illustration) these have the mouth wider than the crown, and follow the outline of the old "saint's hand-bells." I have found three varieties, as follows:

The first is a rather heavy type with flat crown and two staples. The whole surface is covered with minute particles of brass, which suggests that some particular method was employed in making them. When the bells are in use and dirty, this brass is not apparent. The notes of these bells are loud and much more resonant than those of canisters.

The second variety is almost similar in design, but has only one staple, which is placed from front to back. An ordinary strap collar passed through the staple and wedged, is the tackle for this variety.

The third is a much lighter type of bell, similar in metal to the light cluckets. The crown is only a ridge, as in a clucket. Only one substantial staple is fitted to it.

SHEEP-CROOKS AND SHEEP-BELLS 143

At first sight it might be thought that the single staple is a later addition, but a number of the unused bells from the London foundry, shown in Worthing Museum, are of this type.

## *Lewes Bells*

These bells, with very wide mouths, are also made from sheet iron, but differ from all the rest by having the sides *brazed* together instead of being joined by rivets. They were made by Mr. Stephen Lowdell of Lewes, and consequently were known as "Lewes bells."

For a long time I had only one of this kind, but on a visit to Mr. Aucock of Wilmington (described in the notes on brass bells) I obtained another—the smallest one he owned. This is especially interesting as it is one of the few that still retains its original tongue, which is of a peculiar design.

## *Wide-mouthed Brass Bells*

The wide-mouthed brass bell is one of the most uncommon types in Sussex. I have heard these bells referred to as "brass cluckets" and "brass canisters," but both names are misleading, for the bells follow the shape of the wide-mouthed iron ones. I have an excellent specimen which was given to me years ago by Shepherd Harry Coppard of Patcham, although it was the only one he possessed. I have since seen several small ones among the collection of bells belonging to Shepherd Dick Fowler of East Dean. These were used with small latten bells and others on lambs near to the Belle Tout lighthouse.

The most complete collection of them that I have known was owned by Shepherd Charles Funnell of Wilmington. There were originally eighteen in the set, but he had parted with the two largest ones. The pastures round Priory Farm are no longer made cheerful by the sound of these bells, as they have passed into the possession of Mr. Eldon Wright of Dunton Green, Kent, with whom I went to see Mr. Funnell.

Mr. Aucock, another shepherd, who was born at Alfriston, lived with Mr. Funnell, and on the occasion of our visit an impromptu " bell inspection " was hastily arranged for our benefit. First came Mr. Funnell's brass bells and a big horse bell. Then, to our delight, Mr. Aucock opened a bag and tipped out a collection of canisters, Lewes bells, and tackle. It was a wonderful experience to find two shepherds, living together, with collections of the two most uncommon types of brass and iron bells in their possession. I like my photograph of the scene which greeted us on " bell inspection day "—a simple, homely picture, but a reminder of that kindness so often shown by Sussex shepherds and their families to those enthusiasts who take a sincere interest in the details of the shepherd's life.

*Cup Bells*

" Cup " bells are aptly named, for they are like little inverted cups or bowls. They are fitted with tops or staples of various designs for attaching them to the tackle. They were made in sets, and being cast from bell metal, were made in tune one with another. A set must have made a merry jingle! One old shepherd, referring to his father's set, said: " They was a band of music, an' no mistake! " Another described the notes of the small cups as " dingle-ding, dingle-ding! "

There do not appear to be any complete sets of old cup bells now, but even a few, ringing together, produce a very pleasing effect.

Although I have some which are quite plain, cup bells are generally ornamented with incised lines round them, which vary in number. It is unusual to find a specimen

THE SHEEP-WASH AT PLUMPTON, SUSSEX

*Photo by Dr. Habberton Lulham*

SHEPHERD AND FLOCK AT PYECOMBE POND

*Photo by the Author*

with its original crown ring and tongue, possibly because those parts were rather thin and light.

## Horse Bells or "Latten Bells"

The gradual disappearance of horse teams wearing frames of bells created many opportunities for shepherds to add to their collections. Beautiful old frames have been broken up so that the bells could be mounted for use on sheep, and many lots of clucks and dull-sounding bells were made more cheerful by the addition of this type of bell. Some shepherds were tempted to acquire a lot, and one man, who has now left the county, succeeded in collecting a large number and used them all on one flock. The result was a deafening jangle. The old-fashioned charm of chimes from eighteen bells in frames as the team drew a load was completely lost amid such a din.

Many of these bells are cracked by striking stones and troughs and thus rendered useless. Through this rough treatment their number is gradually diminishing—the sad result of using beautiful bells which were not intended for such a purpose.

The original crown rings and tongues of these team bells were so thin and dainty in design that most of them have worn through and have been replaced with others of stouter make. The initials R.W., or the name R. WELLS, in raised letters, found on the inside of many horse-bells, refer to the maker. Further details are given in the paragraphs relating to crotals, or "rumbler" bells.

## White Latten Bells

Among the "horse" bells used on sheep are sometimes found a few of another type known to shepherds as "white latten bells." These are usually numbered on the crown, showing that they were made in sets, as the horse-bells were. Very little is known about them, but shepherds are eager to retain those they have, as they are very pure in tone, and sound well in the open, especially when mounted on chin-boards.

In appearance these bells approach most nearly to old house-bells, but they are of good silvery metal. Their crowns are somewhat flatter than those of horse-bells, and their rims are thickened with a band, and sometimes ornamented with circular lines.

The note as to tongues and crown rings of horse-bells applies equally to this allied type and specimens with original thin inside fittings are rare.

*Crotals or Rumblers.*

I have known only three instances of the use of these bells on sheep in Sussex.

The crotal is an ancient type of bell which has survived until the present day. Small specimens are still found occasionally on horse harness. I have been told that they were mostly used as cattle-bells, and I own a large one (4½ inches in diameter) found on Newmarket Hill near Falmer, which still has an iron fitting attached to hold a broad strap such as is used for a large cow-bell.

In the *Sussex County Magazine* for August, 1929, is a photograph by Mr. D. Merrett of three large crotals (or "rumblers" as the shepherds call them), fitted in a frame similar to those made for horse-bells, and Mr. Arthur Hemming, of Headcorn, Kent, informed me that four similar hoods, which he possesses, were worn by oxen.

"Rumbler" seems a good name for a large crotal, for the note is peculiar and is caused by the continuous rolling of a small iron ball inside. In old specimens this movement has not only worn away the edges of the slit under the bell, but has also caused the iron ball to wear into an irregular shape, consequently much less sound is given than when the bells were new. A glance at the slit, the iron ball, and the hole in the flat appendage to the crown will show whether a specimen is old or modern.

The initials R. W. incised on these bells (which are also found inside many team bells) stand for Robert Wells, the bell maker of Aldbourne, Wiltshire (1764 to 1825). Messrs. Mears & Stainbank, of the Whitechapel Bell Foundry, London, who took over the foundry at Aldbourne in 1825, have the original patterns of these " sleigh bells " and use them at the present time.

Shepherds who have few bells and wish in vain for more, do not despise the ordinary old-fashioned house-bell, nor do they throw away a broken bell if it can be utilised in any way. Strange specimens are found. One used by Mr. Newell on Dyke Hill was half of a large crotal or " rumbler," fitted with a crown ring and tongue. Another which Mr. Nelson Coppard had among an odd lot he purchased was strange to both of us. Eventually we discovered that it was the top part of a large horse-bell fitted with a little tongue.

I have found the study of sheep-bells a fascinating one, for apart from interest in actual specimens the collector gradually understands and shares that deep regard which the shepherds have for their simple treasures.

Of all the bell music heard on the hills the songs of canisters are most charming. More tuneful than clucks or other iron bells, yet not severely correct in tone like cast bells, the canister's mellow notes have a strangely captivating sound. To hear the chimes as their wearers go eagerly homewards across the Downs is to capture a fadeless impression which breeds a desire to enjoy such pleasure again.

## Tackle for Sheep-bells

A glance at the illustrations of bells shows that several kinds of "tackle" are used for fastening them on the sheep's necks, and although quaint little fittings are occasionally found, the tackle in general use is made to more or less standard designs.

At first sight this bell tackle may appear an unimportant item, but the fact that the various parts were always made by the shepherds and could not be purchased at shops, is enough to create interest in such specimens of hand-work.

All the usual items in a shepherd's gear are necessities, but his bells are an optional addition; and although they have a definite use they often prove to be his one hobby.

In past days shepherds collected them and found such pleasure in their possession that they spent many hours of their short leisure in making carefully finished tackle for favourite specimens. It was no tiresome task, but "a matter of personal pride and delight in the job" as one man expressed it. So careful and so thorough was the work in these yokes, pegs, and chin-boards, that some have lasted forty or fifty years. The original sharpness of outline and the marks of the knife have been nearly worn away by the daily rubbing by leather straps and greasy wool, until wood and bone have that smoothness and softness which only age and constant use can produce.

Care of the bells and the making of tackle for them has been a matter of such importance in the lives of many shepherds that I have made a few notes regarding the various methods adopted.

### *Wooden Yokes*

Sheep-bells were often suspended by straps from wooden yokes, made from pieces of branches of trees.

Yew was the favourite wood on account of its toughness and lasting quality. The sharply bent branches of yew trees provided many arched pieces suitable for the purpose. Other kinds of wood were used when yew was not obtainable, also juniper and furze branches, but the softer kinds were not very satisfactory.

These wooden yokes, often referred to as " wooden crooks," passed through several stages before they were completed. After being kept and seasoned in the rough state they were split or chopped into as flat a shape as possible. Sometimes a thick piece of branch could be split in half and made into two crooks. Holes or slots for straps to pass through were made, sometimes by cutting, sometimes by boring or burning, and were finished off with a knife. The careful knife-work then commenced. A hard new yoke took some time to finish off, chip by chip. Occasionally the shepherd's initials were carved on the " crook," and in some cases numbers (probably referring to the number of the bell in a set) are found. Less frequent are carvings of dates and devices. I have three yew crooks which are marked : (1) H.K. 1863 ; (2) 1887 with a star on either side and (3) 1888 with a flag and a cross.

A coat of paint in farm-cart colours, bright red or blue, was the finishing touch. Many old yokes still show some patches of red or blue paint, or traces of both, for at one time it was customary to renew this once a year when bells and tackle were overhauled. Yokes were then threaded on a wire and hung up before being painted. Referring to this a man said to me : " I don't know how 'twas, but there seemed to be time for everything those days ! What with old 'uns an' noo 'uns, I always had a tidy row of 'em on the wire. Some was blue an' some was red, an' once I painted some in stripes, blue *and* red, but I altered 'em nex' time ! "

## Leather Yokes

Inability to acquire suitable branches for " crooks " led many shepherds to adopt an easier plan. Thick pieces of harness leather were trimmed to shape and slots cut without much effort. Such yokes are common, being easy to renew at any time, but they have no charm like the old wooden ones. They are not painted. They are frequently referred to as " collars," and the term " crook " is reserved for the yoke made from a bent branch.

## Strap Collars

A strap collar, usually known as a " strap," is the simplest form of bell tackle. It is just a stout buckle strap with a little hole cut out to receive the top of a bell. Horse and latten bells, crotals and one kind of cup bell, all of which have a little flat appendage with a hole in it on the top of the crown, are easily mounted in this way. The bell-top is pushed through the hole in the strap and secured with a split-pin.

Bells with two staples are occasionally mounted by putting the staples through a slit in a buckle strap and securing them with pegs. In course of time the staples wear deep grooves in the wooden pegs.

Buckle straps are used for most bells with one staple set from front to back. If necessary wedges of leather or a wooden peg, or both, keep the bell in position.

## Chin Boards

The rough-and-ready method of fixing certain bells to a strap collar with a split-pin did not satisfy the shepherds who made their own wooden yokes and pegs. They cut out " chin-boards," which were small pieces of strong wood (generally oak) about six inches by three. A small hole in the centre was shaped to take the flat pierced appendage on the bell-head and a split-pin above the board held the bell tightly. A leather or iron washer was used under the pin if required.

Two varieties of chin board are known to me. The first has two slits cut through it (one each end), and is used on a stout buckle strap which passes through and under it, between it and the bell. The second variety has four holes (two each end), and straps are threaded through before being hung from a yoke.

When I acquired my first chin-board a shepherd told me that in his young days it was customary to use pieces of oak palings for making them. " They was good palin's then," he said, " made o' good oak. There was mos' times a few bits broked off, lyin' 'bout, if so be you wanted some." Then he remarked drily: " Nobody seemed to know how 'twas the tops o' palin's snapped off, an' nobody looked for the bits under the sheepses' necks ! "

I have one chin board, made by Mr. Newell of Devil's Dyke Hill, which is cut from a thick piece of leather instead of oak.

Bells mounted on chin boards not only stay in position, but give sharper, clearer notes when jerked, as the sheep are feeding, than those which dangle from straps.

## *Bell Straps*

Straps used for hanging bells from yokes call for passing comment. They vary in width and thickness, according to the sizes of the staples and slots through which they pass. Sometimes a second (but much shorter) pair are put inside them for greater strength and rigidity. The four thicknesses of leather are then bound round with string or fine wire. Occasionally longer straps are used, being threaded through the bell staples twice instead of once.

## Reeders

Reeders are rough leather "washers" sometimes used between a yoke and the peg to make a bell hang level. Any difference between the length of the two straps or the curve of the two ends of a yoke is thus corrected, and the bell hangs comfortably on the neck of the sheep.

## Lockyers

Lockyers are the pegs which hold the straps to collars and yokes. They are mostly of wood, sometimes of bone, and occasionally of leather. The latter are merely makeshifts, but those of wood and bone claim a share of the interest given to old wooden yokes, for the oldest ones, deeply grooved with wear, and polished by years of use, have a charm of their own.

As in the case of yokes, yew was preferred for lockyers, and some specimens have lasted many years. They were cut out with a knife by shepherds. The rougher modern pegs are poor things by comparison.

Bone lockyers were cut from rib bones with the aid of a vice and saw. Such work was only undertaken by those who took pride in their bells and tackle, and they were pleased to secure good bones for the purpose. Quality of bone and workmanship vary in different specimens. I have some so beautifully made that after many years' daily use they are as smooth and pleasant to handle as ivory.

The two deep grooves in the "waists" of lockyers are cut out very gradually by the movement of the straps round them.

Some of the set of brass bells at Wilmington already mentioned were fitted with long *single* straps, twisted and pegged through strap collars with bone pegs, consequently all these pegs have only a single groove cut in them and are an interesting variety.

All old lockyers are worn with a slight hollow on the under side which has rested and rubbed on the leather or wooden yoke. As they were designed according to the material used, and to the fancy of the maker, many varieties of shape are found, especially in those of yew wood. Although each one was made as an essential part of certain bell tackle, a collection of them is now of great interest, simply as an example of the careful handwork of the oldest shepherds.

My interview with Mr. Blann records his remarks on the making of yokes and lockyers. The quaint little saw is over a hundred years old. Mr. Blann inherited it from his grandfather, who was a wheelwright at Sompting. The work was done mostly in the evening, but a little of it could sometimes be finished off while on the hills with the sheep.

If any excuse be needed for such a long chapter on the details of old sheep-bells and tackle, the record is surely justified by the fact that these things played such an important part in the lives of many shepherds. Bells were useful ; bells were company ; bells provided a good reason for a hobby and an outlet for industry and keen interest which sweetened the hours of duty. The planning of well-finished home-made tackle for them brought into the shepherds' lives the secret satisfaction of the collector, and the pride of the craftsman in work done for pleasure, and for this reason bells and tackle deserve their due share of space in any record of the lives of the the men to whom they meant so much. The old shepherds have so little to leave behind them that these carved pegs, yokes, and chin boards will be treasured one day as specimens of their work.

## SHEARING, ETC.

"I ANSWERS a tidy lot o' queshuns one way an'-nother these days," said a shepherd who had once been a member of a shearing gang. "People mos' time stops for a few words ef they be nigh 'nough."

It appeared that his crook was the chief item of interest with most people, then the bells, then the dog. "But t'other day," he said, "there wur a man askin' 'bout songs an' things at sheep-shearin's; 'e asked ef it warnt a jolly time! 'Well, yes,' I says, 'the singin' part was jolly 'nough, far's 't goes, but t' rest was d——d 'ard work, an' thet's the truth! But us looked forrard to it all the same,' I says, 'for 'twas a *change*, an' us didun get much changes 'ceptin' at fair times an' such.'"

Then the shepherd glanced away across the Downs, but I don't think he saw anything at all at that moment, for he suddenly said: "Yes! I'd like jus' one more o' they ol' Black Ram nights agin, thet I would—but I won't never get it!"

The apparent ease with which a shepherd performs many duties such as pitching or carrying hurdles on his shoulders reveals hidden strength, but the shearing of forty sheep a day is no light task. "'Tis a back-aching ol' job," said one man, who does the work with one assistant, "but we knows as 'twill come. The wool grows, an' mus' be sheared off, an' there 'tis!"

So much interest attaches to the details of the old sheep-shearings that the actual hard work, the tiring bending, and the relief of putting the shears in the pouch at the end of the day's work is more or less overlooked in most accounts, just as these things were ignored and temporarily forgotten by the shearers while their evening meals and sing-songs were in progress.

The following notes are compiled from details supplied by men who took part in the shearings.

The shearing gang, varying in number from ten to twenty or more, was in charge of one man, known as the Captain. His right-hand man was known as the Lieutenant, and they were distinguished by the bands worn round their hats—a gold one for the Captain, and a silver one for his assistant.

The Captain was an able man, capable of making arrangements with farmers for shearings, acting as treasurer, and attending to all the little details connected with the trips of the gang. His ability was apparent on the night of the first meeting at an appointed inn. This was known as "White Ram" night. The proceedings started with a shilling subscription for a supply of beer (provided for the shearers at the rate of a shilling a gallon). Shepherds and others who wished to join the party were allowed to do so, and they subscribed the same amount.

The programme of work was made known, and by arrangement between the Captain and certain vendors packets of sheep-shears of varying weights were on sale. Shearers could select a new pair if required, and could either pay cash or settle for them at the last meeting. Shepherds were also allowed to purchase shears at the same time.

When the gang arrived at a farm where the Captain had contracted to shear the flock for so much a score (and beer) they found everything in readiness. In fine weather shearing was often carried out in the open, otherwise in a barn. Sometimes ground-sheets were laid down for convenience, so that stray pieces of wool could be collected easily and included with the fleeces, and all the wool kept in clean condition.

"Catchers" were on duty to fetch sheep from a handy pen, or "hopper," to the shearers as required. Shears were soon busy, and fleeces were skilfully rolled up by the "winder," who was generally an old man past heavy work, such as a day's shearing.

In the picture (given to me by a shepherd) is a view of the shearing ground at Saddlescombe Farm, about 1888. The group includes the shepherd, his wife, the winder, two catchers, twelve shearers and the "tar-boy." The latter was the youngest member of the party, ready for instant attendance upon the shearers when required. The sudden struggling movements of sheep under the shearer's hands often result in a tiny cut on the skin. In olden days a dab of tar was put on with the finger or a stick, but later a pinch of lime was used to cover in the wound, so that the dreaded pest, the fly, should not be enticed to settle on it. Any shearer who required the tar called: "Tar-boy!" who immediately answered: "Coming up, sir!" When lime was used the old name, like the tar, stuck to the boys employed for the purpose. Other duties of a "tar-boy" were the sweeping of bits of wool from the sheet and the fetching of more beer whenever it was required.

Young shearers in their first season (and sometimes the second, too) were termed "colts." They were supposed to wind their own fleeces. In this way they not only learned their work, but were "kept in their place" in the gang.

In the foreground of the picture is what appears to be a fine Sussex-ware pitcher with two mugs. This pitcher contained oatmeal water and lemon, but in the usual way a supply of mild beer known as "swanky" was provided for shearing gangs, also a meal in the middle of the day.

After the day's work the men had more food and stronger ale. The Sheep Shearing Song was sung and the evening spent in relaxation after such tiring work—smoking, drinking, and singing old songs appreciated by shearers and shepherds. Many shearers carried their own horn cups with them. Mr. Jesse Moulding, of Goring, has the specimen used successively by his great-grandfather, grandfather and father, and this yellow-coloured " horn " is a treasured possession.

When all the shearing trips were over for the season another gathering was held at the inn. This was called " Black Ram " night. The Captain of the gang made the final share-out, and money owing for shears was paid. Each member contributed again to the general fund and a convivial evening followed.

*Note.*—Miss Maude Robinson, who lived at the famous Saddlescombe Farm, was surprised to see the picture of the shearing gang, and informed me that it was one of a series taken for her by a Hurstpierpoint photographer. She was not aware that anyone else owned a copy, but her gift to Nelson Coppard had been hidden in the shepherd's box for many years with other treasures. (Nelson may be seen in the picture, wearing a white hat.) Miss Robinson invited me to her home in Brighton to see the old Sussex-ware pitcher which is still intact, and many other interesting links with the old days at Saddlescombe Farm.

## SUSSEX SHEEP-SHEARING SONG

Come all my jolly boys, and we'll together go
About with our Captain, to shear the lamb and ewe,[1]
In the merry month of June, of all times in the year,
'Tis always the season the ewe and lambs to shear ;
And then we must work hard, boys, until our backs do ache
And our master he will bring us beer whenever we do lack.

[1] Pronounced " Yo."

Our master he comes round to see our work is doing well,
And he cries " Shear them close, men, for there is but little wool."
" Oh, yes, good master," we reply, " we'll do well as we can,"
When our Captain calls " Shear close, boys," to each and every man;
And at some places still we have this story all day long,
" Shear them well and close, boys," and this is all their song.

And then our noble Captain doth unto our master say
" Come, let us have one bucket of your good ale, I pray."
He turns unto our Captain, and makes him this reply :
" You shall have the best of beer, I promise, presently."
Then out with the bucket pretty Betsy she doth come,
And master says " Maid, mind and see that every man has some ! "

This is some of our pastime as we the sheep do shear,
And though we are such merry boys we work hard I declare ;
And when 'tis night, and we are done, our master is more free,
And fills us well with good strong beer, and pipes and tobacco ;
And so we do sit and drink, we smoke and sing and roar,
Till we become more merry far than e'er we were before.

When all our work is done, and all our sheep are shorn,
Then home with our Captain to drink the ale that's strong ;
'Tis a barrel then of hum-cup, which we call the " Black Ram,"
And we do sit and swagger, and swear that we are men,
But yet before 'tis night, I'll stand you half a crown
That if you don't have a special care this " Ram " will knock you down !

The old days are dead ; the old ways are dying out. On many farms the shepherd and his assistants now shear the flock with patent clippers worked by a machine.

With these modern appliances the animals are sheared quickly and closely, and as they stand in a crowd waiting for the next victims to join them they look so naked and miserable that they are a dismal sight.

Show flocks are still sheared by hand with the old shears. An even fleece, free from ridges, is thereby ensured, and the sheep do not lose too much wool.

On farms where small flocks are kept the shepherd is expected to manage the shearing by hand in the old way with the help of an assistant.

Small flocks and show flocks therefore provide us with opportunities to watch shearing in the old style—work that is far more fascinating to the onlooker than to those employed.

We may still see the sheep waiting in the hopper, see them sheared and released, and watch the fleeces being wound into a compact bundle. Sometimes we may see a keg of beer, supplied for the shearers, in a corner of the shed. So much is still left to us, but one feature of the old shearings is gone for ever—the very attractive little figure of the tar-boy. " Lowest in the gang, with many masters to please, expecting no praise for instant service (and a kick for anything less) "—such was the word-picture passed on to me ! Instantly my sympathy and interest were centred on him. It seemed quite worth while to arrange an enlargement of the tar-boy from the photo of a shearing gang.

It was my good fortune to meet Mr. Jack Hazelgrove, who, forty years ago, acted as tar-boy to the old Clapham and Patching gang. He told me that they used to start work on the farms at 6.30 a.m., and this often made it necessary to leave home at 4 a.m. From 6.30 onwards, with the exception of dinner time, he was kept busy. He explained to me that tar was not just dabbed on as one might think. It was put on with his finger and as the tar dropped on the wound the finger was turned over and the tar spread with it. At some farms tar was not used, and he was provided with wood ashes. At the call "Tar-boy" he attended, dropped a little wood ash on the wound and spread it gently with his finger.

When intervals for refreshment were announced it was his duty to fill the shearers' mugs with beer, while in his spare minutes he helped the winder, and learned to wind fleeces properly. Later he learned to shear by beginning or finishing ewes, and became a "colt."

When work was over for the day the gang returned home, but occasionally where there was a large flock to shear they would take food for two days. They slept in a barn or cart-shed. After such work a farm waggon lined with fleeces was a welcome bed.

On the long journeys to and fro the most direct paths to outlying farms were used. At other odd times members of the gang would meet for a ramble, and on such occasions it was their pleasure to tread out footpaths and keep them open. By this means Mr. Hazelgrove obtained a wonderful knowledge of the paths and rights of way around the district, and he uses them still. I trod out some of them with him, and feel sure that some of the delightful walks enjoyed by us to-day would probably have been lost if the footpaths had not been trodden out and kept open by members of the old shearing gangs.

The recording of details of shearing and of shearers' songs and beer provides me with an opportunity to gratify a certain old man by including a few further notes.

Old Shepherd F—— is very deaf, which causes him to shout. He bawled to me "I read they books !— I see yew've writ 'bout a 'menjous lot o' things, an' yet, to me, it do sim queer that yew ent writ a piece 'bout de good ol' Sussex beer !" So now I feel I must correct that rather serious fault, although I'm not a proper judge of either hops or malt ;—the drinks I like are

JOHN BEECHER WITH HIS DOGS

*Photos by the Author*

SHEPHERD NEWELL WITH "PRINCE"

*Photo by the Author*

"BREAK 'EM IN YOUNG!" SAID GRANDFATHER

cheap and sweet, while ale is sour and dear—but, just to please old F——, I'll write " a piece " about the beer.

One glorious day, in merry May, the sunbeams scorched my head
As I trudged up a Sompting lane, and reached the shearing shed.
My friend the shepherd, bending low, as men do when they shear;
Called " Mornin' !—come inside—sit down, and draw yourself some beer !"
I filled the old mug to the brim; I drank—and drew some more;
I never had enjoyed a drop of beer like that before !
Since then I've tried, without success, that pleasure to repeat,
And purchased many a brimming mug of ale that was no treat.
The flavour did not even please, nor satisfy, nor cheer
As did that of the precious pint of Sompting shearer's beer.
I love the famous Sussex inns at Alfriston and Rye
And I enjoy their ancient charms more than the drinks I buy.
I find delight in beakers bright that once were filled with ale;
I like horn cups and old brown jugs; they tell me many a tale
Of those who used them in the past; they hold the memories dear
Of men who drank each other's health in good old Sussex beer !

The shepherd's bag, which is carried to and fro each day, usually contains a bottle of drink—sometimes tea or other mild beverage and sometimes ale. Old F—— confessed to me that a drop of ale was his favourite drink when he was on the hills, but he never indulged in strong beer while at work. " It do get a hold of yew in time," he said, and he quoted an instance of two friends of his. One drank ale and lived to be eighty-odd, but the other, who always drank strong beer, came to an untimely end, and the thought of him had been a good lesson to F——. He referred to the fact that mild ale was provided for the shearing gangs, which merely helped them to continue their strenuous task. He also referred to the potent effect of the beer drunk by some of the gang on " Black Ram " night, when the shearing was over.

At fairs and sheep sales it is usual for farmers who are selling to treat their shepherds to some drink during the hours they stand by the pens, or to give them money for that purpose. In addition to this it was customary at some places for the head of the auctioneering firm to provide free beer to those shepherds in charge of the sheep. The reason for the abrupt stoppage of this custom at one fair ground was related to me, in confidence, as I stood chatting by a fold. It appears that D——, an East Sussex shepherd, was known as a man who enjoyed his beer, and his capacity for carrying it made others envious. With other shepherds he attended the booth for the usual free beer. It was given to them in a large jug, which was emptied and returned in due course. D—— was still thirsty. He said to the others : " It do seem a pity they should take any o' that beer away again, boys ! Us ought to be smart enough to get another jug, surelye ! " and he suggested a novel plan for obtaining it. Under his direction a few of them (as much for fun as for an extra drink) disguised themselves in odd hats and garments borrowed from other members of the company; sauntered to the booth and asked for beer. They were ready to give other men's names if asked. To their surprise the beer was handed over. Their success induced others to try the same method, but, unknown to them, certain eyes and tongues had been busy, with dire result. Since that day there has been no more free beer supplied by that auctioneer !

Here is an old song which was included in the programme following the "Sheep-Shearing Song." According to the singer it was a general favourite. Like many another old country song it may differ by a line or two from other versions (a certain amount of licence being allowed to the singers), but it is easy to believe that the shearers made the most of their opportunity to join in the simple chorus.

## A DROP OF GOOD BEER

I'm Roger Rough the ploughman,
A ploughman, sir, am I;
Just like my thirsty father
My throttle's always dry!
The world goes round—to me 'tis right,
With no one I interfere,
But I'll sing and work from morn till night,
And then I will drink my beer!

*Chorus:*
I likes a drop o' good beer, I doos,
I'm fond of a drop o' good beer, I is,
Let gentlemen fine set down to their wine
And I will stick to my beer!

There's Sally—that's my wife, sir—
Likes beer as well as me,
And seems as happy in life, sir,
As a woman could seem to be;
She minds her home, takes care of the tin—
No gossiping idlers near;
Sure as every Saturday night comes round,
Like me she drinks her beer!

There's my old dad—God bless him!—
He's now turned ninety-five;
No work could ever depress him,
He's the happiest man alive!

He's old in age, but young in health,
His heart and hand both clear!
Possessed of those he keeps good health,
But still he sticks to his beer!

Now lads, need no persuasion,
But send your glasses round,
And never fear invasion
While barley grows on our grounds.
May discord cease, and trade increase
With every coming year—
When everything's crowned, and counts all paid,
Then I'll sing and drink my beer!

In Shepherd Michael Blann's old song-book I found the words of a good song in praise of beer. It was written for him by his brother and that was all he knew about it. Later Mr. Arthur Beckett informed me that most of it was taken from a collection of verses by John Hollamby of Hailsham, published in *Our Sussex Parish* by Thomas Geering. A copy of the song, as I found it, is given below.

### BLANN'S BEER

Oh, " Blanns " is the beer for me ;
  A pint of it's so handy,
It is as fine as any wine
  And strong as any brandy!

If you are ill 'twill make you well
  And put you in condition ;
A man that will drink Blann's old ale
  Has need of no physician!

*Chorus:*
Oh, Blann's is the beer for me, etc.

'Twill fill your veins and warm your brains
  And drive out melancholy ;
Your nerves 'twill brace, and paint your face,
  And make you fat and jolly.

The foreigners may praise their wines !—
  'Tis only to deceive us !
Would they come here and taste this beer
  I'm sure they'd never leave us !

The meagre French their thirst would quench,
  And find much good 'twould do them ;—
Keep them a year on Blann's good beer,
  Their country would not know them.

All you that have not tasted it,
  I'd have you set about it ;
No man with pence and common sense
  Would ever be without it !

I will finish my " piece " about beer by recording the fact that I have never seen a drunken shepherd, although I know many who " like their pint." The word " pint " made me think again of Charlie X——, who liked " a drop of good beer " and the story of him will show that he was worth a few pages to himself.

### The Merry Shepherd

I never look at my pictures of old Charlie X——, who was one of the East Sussex shepherds, without a feeling of amusement. My visit to his home, in company of some mutual friends, made the day a memorable one. I not only acquired a sheep-bell and some bell-tackle of special interest, but also enjoyed the shepherd's company when he was off duty and in a particularly entertaining mood.

I think that Charlie must have been blamed so often for what he did and what he did not do that he ceased to care for anybody's opinion, and I have more than a suspicion that his reputation as a judge of beer provided him with an excellent excuse for extra fun. He was no longer young, but the spirit of mischief was in his brown eyes, and the little creases in his dark face indicated a tendency to merriment which could not be suppressed.

We were a party of five round the dinner-table—four men and the wife of another shepherd (whom Charlie called "Mother"). "I've had a nice little drop o' good beer," began Charlie, but he was stopped, for Mother appeared with a large steak pudding, greens, potatoes, and carrots. Our plates were generously filled as if we were all shepherds. It was not a meal to linger over, but Charlie found time to endeavour to choke us all, and to record his regret that so much good beer still remained in the barrel at the inn. With knife and fork poised above his plate he said: "I wondered if I should have time to drink a pint before you came along, but I finished it up. Then I looks out o' 'The Lion' door, but you wasn't in sight, and I thinks to myself '*shall* I have time for another pint?' and I thinks 'yes, I *might* do it!'—and just as I was turning to get it I saw you come along. I only had one very nice pint—I wish it had been more, because——" Mother's eyes met those of old Charlie and he hastily resumed his meal.

Our first course being finished, Mother cleared away plates and dishes to make room for plums and custard, and Charlie started off again. "I don't know, gentlemen, what *you* thought about that pudding, but I've had better!—the meat in it seemed rather tough!" We looked at each other in surprise, for the dinner was perfectly served, but the voice continued: "The carrots warn't done, and the greens was done too much, and as for the taters!"—The pantry door moved, and Mother appeared. "What was the matter with the potatoes?" she demanded. "It's all right, Mother," replied the shepherd, with affected meekness, "I was just saying what a lovely dinner it was! Such a good pudding! and the carrots was beautiful!" Mother's quick glance was sufficient to show that she knew all there was to know.

The plums and custard proved to be as good as the first course. "I always count my stones," observed Charlie. "I may be lucky to-day!" As soon as he could he repeated old phrases. His luck was still out, but his comments and fresh references to beer amused us. At length we rose, and I was about to move my chair when Charlie clutched it. (I wondered why.) "*I'll* put the chair back," he said. Moving quite nimbly, he planted it in the corner with one leg in the cat's dinner-plate. Mother saw it, and chided him, but he said: "I'm sorry, Mother!" in such a grieved tone that he deceived me for a moment. Then he remarked: "Wrong again! There oughtn't to be plates of dinner sitting on the floor! What people want to put plates of dinner on the floor for I *don't* know. The chair always *does* stand in that corner, and I——" "Oh, don't talk so much," exclaimed Mother (but she turned away to smile). The old shepherd's voice began again: "Wrong again!" he said, in a mournful tone, "always wrong! When I talks I'm told to be quiet, and when I'm quiet somebody says: 'Why don't you talk?' If I sit and look in the fire, *that* isn't right. 'What you want to look in the fire for? Haven't you got *anything* to say?' If I look up the chimney for a bit, *that* isn't right either. 'What you looking up chimney for? Don't you feel well?' 'Tis enough to make *anyone* go to 'The Lion' for a pint!" Then he smiled suddenly and his eyes twinkled as he opened the door. "If you are ready, gentlemen, we will walk over the hill to the fold, and get an appetite for tea." We collected our hats and sticks and went outside. The old tease stepped back to the door and called "Good-bye, Mother dear!" like a repentant child.

# SHEEP-WASHING, MARKING, AND COUNTING

## Sheep-washing

THE heavy work of washing sheep thoroughly in cold water a week or more previous to shearing was an additional duty in former days. Farmers were naturally eager to see their wool put on the market in the cleanest and best condition possible, as clean " clips " fetched far better prices.

The practice has now died out in most districts. Wool staplers now prefer unwashed fleeces, as lanoline is extracted from them by a special process. This was formerly washed out of the wool and wasted in the sheep-wash.

So many farms lacked a brook with a deep pool, or any other place suitable for a wash, that many flocks were driven to appointed spots every year for the purpose. One of these places was Fulking, where the remains of the old sheep-wash, beside the Shepherd and Dog Inn, can still be inspected. The following description is reprinted from *Sussex in Bygone Days*, being the reminiscences of a well-known surgeon, Mr. Nathanial P. Blaker, who was brought up at Perching, in the same district.

" Fulking, in times when the number of sheep kept on the South Downs was far greater than at present (1906), was a place to which all the flocks within a somewhat large radius were sent to be washed ; for it is necessary to wash sheep before they are shorn in order to remove the gritty material, which would not only deteriorate the quality of the wool, but would also blunt the edge of the shears. Fulking, besides its central position as far as the Southdown flocks were concerned, was admirably fitted for the construction of a place for washing sheep. A spring of pure water, one of several which issue at irregular intervals from the front of the South Downs, rises here, and soon cuts its way through some rising ground, which forms a bank on each side, and so, by constructing a dam by some very simple appliances, the water could be raised to any required height. A small pen or fold, of which the stream formed one side, was constructed, capable of holding twenty or thirty sheep, and into this the sheep were driven. From this pen they were thrown into the water and washed by two or three men who stood in the stream and were for several hours up to their waists in the cold water; and though the sheep-washing took place in May or June, the water, as it issued from the hill, was bitterly cold. The flock itself was kept in a larger pen, one side of which was formed by that of the sheep-wash itself; the opposite side by a post and rail fence, and each end by the same sort of fence and a gate. Through these two gates the main high road passed, so that during the time the sheep were being washed, the high road was stopped, and when a cart or other vehicle appeared, it was held up until a man could open the gate at each end and allow it to pass. Such was the primitive state of things in those days. There were but few railways, their influence on the habits of the people was not yet felt, and there was none of the hurry of modern times. The amount of traffic was very small, generally only two or three carts in a day. Even a stranger on the road was so rare that people turned round and stared after he had passed, and so it was a somewhat rare event for the sheep-wash gates to be opened and the sheep disturbed, and when it happened the drivers took it as a matter of course.

"To stand for hours up to the waist in a stream of cold water was most trying work for the men who washed the sheep, and I have seen them, when the work was over, walk to the 'Shepherd and Dog,' the adjacent public house, stiff and scarcely able to move with cold, and with the water dripping from them and sprinkling the ground like a shower of rain. They suffered much from rheumatism in various forms, and could only continue the work for a very few years. For several years before the sheep-wash was closed the men stood in casks fixed in the ground in the stream."[1]

From shepherds who once drove their flocks to Fulking I have learned that the washpool was hired from the farmer by those who undertook the work. These men charged so much a score, or so much a hundred, for washing, and paid the farmer a proportion of the total. The farmer provided posts, rails and faggots for making the pens and folds, and kept the sheep-wash in repair.

"I remember the last I saw of it," said Nelson Coppard; "there were two men in tubs to wash the sheep, two to throw the sheep in, and another standing by with a dipping-hook. Sometimes it was touch-and-go with a sheep if you hadn't a hook handy. Once when our lot were waiting to go in I spotted a ewe among those in the pen that didn't look to me as if she were fit to go in. Just then I was sent to the 'Shepherd and Dog' for beer, and when I came back they were pulling her out of the water—dead."

[1] By permission of Messrs. Combridge of Hove.

Another shepherd said to me: "It were a rare job, this washing, but I used to like to see my flock so nice and clean for the shearing. The men who stood in the water and washed them had a cold job! They were kept busy with big flocks such as we had then, and whatever they got for the washing, I reckon they earned it!"

During a chat with George Bailey, who was shepherd at Beeding Court Farm for forty-six years, I was amused by the tale of a certain man whom he knew.

When speaking of Fulking and sheep-washing he recalled a lively occurrence at another wash where he attended with his flock. It had been the usual practice to run the sheep on to the lawn before the house of the man who owned the wash-pool, but on this occasion he shut the gate and refused to allow it. As the shepherd explained to me, "if a man let out a sheep-wash he was supposed to have room for the sheep." It was very unreasonable, and the washers took strong exception to his sudden action. Further friction occurred when he claimed the wool collected from the water. The men thereupon threatened to throw him in the wash. "He came and stood by me on the brickwork," said Mr. Bailey, "and complained to me. 'They threatened to throw me in the wash!' he said, so *I* said, 'Yes, I'd like to do it myself!' 'Ah!' he shouted, 'you're all a clique together! I won't have it! I'll send for the policeman!' He did so," continued Mr. Bailey. "The policeman came, but the fun commenced when he tried to take the names! One man had forgotten his name, another had never had a name, the next had sold his name to someone else, and so on!" The upshot of it was that the case came before the court and two of the men were fined a shilling each, "which just shows," said the shepherd, "that they were not really in the wrong."

## Sheep-Marking

In an interview with Shepherd Walter Wooler, I recorded the process of marking sheep with the farmer's initial, which is printed in pitch on the wool with a marking iron. In addition we find many sheep with dots of colour on them in various parts of the body. These marks, usually dabbed on with the end of a stick, may denote sex in lambs, but in the case of sheep they are the cryptic signs by which the shepherd keeps his records and sorts his flock.

At sheep sales buyers may often be seen putting their own mark on animals just purchased.

Every sheep born in a registered Southdown flock and retained for breeding is tattooed with the official trade mark of the Southdown Sheep Society, and its breeder's registered flock number. This mark is tattooed in the left ear during the animal's first year, and before it leaves its breeder's possession. It is done with a specially made marking tool.

The ear is the usual place for permanent marking; consequently many ears are seen perforated with small holes, or with snicks of various designs cut out of the edges. These marks, made by punches, are mostly used to denote ages, and are a more reliable guide than the teeth of the animals.

In an eighteenth-century copy of the *Sussex Weekly Advertiser*, Mr. Arthur Beckett found an advertisement offering a reward for some sheep which had strayed and which were marked with "a farthing in the ear." At that date I had no information on the matter, but I made enquiries and discovered that George Humphrey of Sompting knew all about it. The details were published in the *Sussex County Magazine*, and are summarised below:

When he was a boy his father owned a little marking

iron made from a farthing. The coin being drilled with a small hole, a metal rod was pointed and put through hot, and clamped. A little wooden handle was fitted to the rod. This made a very "pretty" tool and as the coin chosen was a new one it gave a good neat impression when used to mark a sheep with a dot of black or colour (as is done now). The greater the care in touching the farthing with the paint the neater the mark was, and as it was customary then with their beautiful Southdown flock of 400 to give great attention to detail and neatness in every way, the farthing iron was a treasured possession.

Shepherd Humphrey remembers his father's grief when the tool was lost. The occurrence caused him to question his father about it and he learned that the grandfather had taught his father how to use it. Another new farthing was procured and a home-made iron was produced.

Apart from ordinary marking the farthing iron was used to mark sheep inside the ear. This mark was known as a "memorandum mark." It was, in fact, a secret mark for the shepherd's own use. Two instances of its particular value for marking are given:

(1) Ewes that gave particular trouble at lambing time would be likely to do the same again. These were marked in the ear with the farthing and were included in those set apart for sale to a butcher.

(2) Where several rams were kept together for convenience, as was done on their farm, his father's rams were marked in the ear by him, thus settling any argument as to their ownership when the time came to sort them out.

At a later date another shepherd, Walter Wooler, of Pyecombe, told me that he could confirm the above details, as he remembered a "farthing" marking tool being used.

The interview with Nelson Coppard records another method of marking by the use of "earings,"—small metal tickets fastened to the ear by a ring.

### Sheep-counting

Anyone who is unaccustomed to the quick counting of moving sheep finds it less easy than they would expect to arrive at the correct number.

The average shepherd is used to such work, and as the animals crowd closely and rush through the small space opened for them between two hurdles, his eyes and brain work quickly, and as the last one scampers through he is ready with his total. I have only known of two exceptions to the general rule. These men both owned that the sight of the sheep passing by rapidly turned them giddy. One of them, when a boy, was so affected by dizziness at these times that he fell "all of a heap." He was not of much use at the work for many years.

The origin of the quaint sets of numerals used in various parts of the country by shepherds and drovers has been the cause of much speculation among philologists. Apart from the possible sources of derivation of certain words, it seems to be a generally accepted fact that the system of counting by these special scores must have been handed down from remote times, although the exact forms may have changed.

Through the kindness of Mr. H. Walford Lloyd I am able to quote an authentic instance of the use of a curious set of numerals in Sussex. In a letter to me he referred to an old farmer of Slindon, near Arundel, who had started life as a shepherd lad under another well-known farmer in the same district. His letter includes an entertaining account of suppers with the old farmer, and of subsequent cosy hours by a log fire while he listened to tales of sheep and shepherding. The following extract is valuable as a record:

"He [the farmer] told me that one job was 'telling' the sheep. The sheep were allowed to run through a hurdle, *two at a time*, and, as the boy, he had to stand there and count them, keeping time with the shepherd, thus:

>One-erum
>Two-erum
>Cockerum
>Shu-erum
>Shitherum
>Shatherum
>Wine-berry
>Wagtail
>Tarrydiddle
>Den

—that 'Den' meaning a score, or twenty sheep through the hurdle."

Recording of sheep scores on "tally sticks" was once usual in Sussex, and specific instances have been noted. Although I have not been lucky enough to find any specimens, some of the shepherds I have met have used them. One man referred to them, and said: "Most times I used my crook-stick to cut the notches in, so I never lost my count. 'Tis a handy way if you beant much of a scholar. Pencil an' paper be good in their way too, but not as good as a stick an' a knife; the notches is allus to hand, an' easy to remember."

## DEW-PONDS, AND OTHERS

THERE is some fascination to most of us in the sight of a dew-pond. To those who find one unexpectedly while rambling on the hills it offers a pleasant little thrill. To bird lovers it is a place where many feathered friends may be met. To those who have made a particular study of the subject it is merely a specimen of some pond-maker's work, either clay puddled or chalk puddled, with cemented margin or chalk margin, and so on, but to the shepherd and sheep a good dew-pond is just a blessing.

The fact that chapters and volumes of facts concerning these ponds have been written is a matter of indifference to most shepherds, although the elements of mystery surrounding the exact cause for an unfailing supply of water in some of them may appeal to the men more than they will admit. I have already recorded how one shepherd who was cross-questioned by a visitor, to his great annoyance, said: "I never seed onyone a-fillin' 'un up, so I don't know nought 'bout it!" Only once have I received a decided answer from a shepherd on this point. In reply to my question he said: "What fills 'em?—Well, I reckon 'tis rain an' mistes, *but don't say as I said so!*" The word had evidently gone round among the shepherds that this matter, which could not be decided definitely, was being probed.

The main interest to them is the usefulness of the pond for watering; the main fact is that if no pond be available other arrangements must be made, which may mean longer journeys to water or extra work in filling troughs by a pump. It is no joke to pump up water for a flock of three or four hundred, especially with apparatus which is old or imperfect. At a Pyecombe farm the refusal of a steward to have a pump repaired caused the shepherd hours of work in hot weather. He had to haul water up from an underground reservoir in a bucket, pour it into a tank, and transfer it again to a pipe leading to the troughs. What a blessing a dew-pond would have been to this old man!

In the absence of proof it is still uncertain whether such ponds were constructed in Stone Age days by trampling out or other easy means, although, whatever the process employed, it is reasonable to presume that provision was made for the watering of flocks and herds. Mr. H. S. Toms has a store of details relating to his researches on old pond sites, and records of pits apparently used for water storage, one of which he found near a kitchen-midden at Belle Tout near Eastbourne.

Mr. Edward A. Martin records the fact that dew-ponds are also known by other names in other counties; namely, mist-ponds, cloud-ponds, and fog-ponds. Our shepherds do not use any particular name as a rule, but refer to them as sheep-ponds, and those who pronounce "sheep" as "ship" say "ship-ponds." While speaking of a period of drought a shepherd said to me: "My bottle o' tea diddun las' me—I had a drink out o' the ship-pond mos' days. I be still alive, so 't seems it diddun hurt me!" Some people are not afraid of pond water. I have seen gipsy women come to the pond on Stanmer Down and take away their daily supply in buckets.

I have often accompanied a shepherd and flock on

their way to a dew-pond, and have always hurried along in front as we neared it, so that I could watch the arrival of the sheep. It is a pleasant sensation to wait, with camera ready, to hear the bells ring as the eager crowd race along. The first heads appear, but by the time the camera is focused a mob have crowded to the pond's edge for a welcome drink. The first, satisfied, stand aside, and others take their place. As the sheep drink, their bells often touch the water. The shepherd and his dog stand by until all are served. As the water settles the forms of the sheep are reflected clearly for a minute, but the surface is soon disturbed again by the dog, who laps quickly, dashes in, dashes out, shakes vigorously, and is ready to round up the flock and direct them again.

A photograph portraying the scene may be a good one, but printed, with appropriate title, it is very tame and unimportant; yet it brings back those few tense moments so full of life—the first ripples on the pond's surface, the eager, pushing throng, the silent shepherd, the dog waiting his turn and watching his master's eyes for the signal to refresh himself, and the songs of the bells as the crowd move away.

Even when a shepherd leads his flock, as some do, he is seldom the first to reach the pond. For this reason it is doubtful whether he sees as much of the wild life as those who go warily towards the pond for the purpose. I have seen two foxes go away, and once a stoat was near the edge, but the latter may have been there on the chance of catching an unsuspecting victim, for many birds come to the ponds, as may be proved by the stray feathers which are left on the margin. Glimpses of retreating animals, of magpies, pigeons, and partridges, and the dropped feathers (including one from a Tawny Owl found at Stanmer Down pond) all suggest that a disguised hut or hiding-place would be productive of a vast amount of dew-pond lore.

We may remember so many alluring items connected with a pond; its reflections of clouds, and of a hovering skylark, the wonderful glow of a sunset which appeared as flames in the water, and the bewitching effect of moonlight on its still surface; yet at the mention of the word "dew-pond" our first thought is of its edge ringed by thirsty sheep with bent heads, and the thought suggests that the familiar scene is only a repetition of similar ones constantly repeated since the days when shepherds first took domesticated flocks to them on the Sussex hills.

## THE SHEPHERD'S COMPANION

SO many of us are dog lovers, and fond of our jolly companions, that we hardly realize how different is the lot of the sheep-dog to that of the ordinary pet. He (or she) is born to a life of responsible work, and shares with the shepherd the care of the flock. Like him, he works every day in the year, and his leisure is very short. The walk towards home at the end of the day is generally his only opportunity for play, and then, if he is not too tired, he may poke about and hunt, or do any of the hundred things which delight him. Occasionally a shepherd, whose own heart beats quicker at the swish of a bird's wings or the sound of some animal in the undergrowth, will allow his four-footed mate a little liberty if occasion offers, but the word *duty* looms so large in front of them both that the shepherd cannot often afford to give the signal for relaxation. More often he finds it necessary to shout: "Come back, you monkey!" or something equally curt, although there are times when such expressions are not a true index to his real feelings.

On meeting old M—— you might think him very gruff, and to hear him shout at his dog you would be tempted to form a rather unfavourable opinion of him, yet you would be mistaken. "I do bawl at that dog," he remarked, "but he do need it, times—I don't know whether I ever *shall* make a good dog of him, but I'm afraid not! It don't do to let him *see* me laughin', but he doos some comical things. Times I bawls at him, but I laughs inside me all t' time. I reckon I be gettin' reg'lar soft—but I bin a nursemaid ev'ry spring fur nigh on seventy year, so p'raps that be somethin' t' do with it!"

A shepherd is obliged to be particularly strict with a young dog in training, hence his impatience with people who feed a sheep-dog or bring other dogs near enough to distract the puppy's attention from the work in hand. It is usual to put a young dog to work with an older and experienced one for a time, but directly it shows an aptitude for work it should be separated from its companion and trained to obey orders alone. " It is a great mistake to leave them together too long," said one man to me, " for if 'tis done the young un is apt to expect to wait for t'other to help, and not *try* to work alone."

It is the careful, patient training of dogs which is responsible for the wonderful work which surprises us. Every shepherd has his own ways, and his dog is used to them, consequently we may see dogs obey signals made by a raised arm, or a motion with a crook, or respond to nods of the shepherd's head, movements of his eyes, whistles, calls, muttered words, and other half-secret signs.

The following incident was related to me by a friend who had been studying the ways of shepherds in connection with a book which he was writing:

" While there was a mist on the hills I went to find Shepherd G——, just for the experience. I wanted to hear unseen sheep bells and to study the details of a shepherd's work at such a time. After much difficulty I located the flock and G——'s collie found me. As you know, he is not a very safe animal. He rushed at me when I appeared, but fortunately did no harm. When I met G—— I told him that I had had difficulty in finding him and that I wished to accompany him in his walk through the mist. To my surprise he asked me to come another day, and on being pressed for an explanation said: ' You see, I want all the work I can get from the dog in this mist. If *you* come he'll be trying to watch you as well as the sheep, and I can't afford to have him attending to anything except his work.'

" Although I was disappointed I could appreciate the shepherd's view of the matter and was glad to have heard his explanation, as it gave me a fresh idea about the work of a sheep-dog."

Some shepherds show a preference for bob-tails or similar rough-haired dogs, others for collies. Both kinds are seen at sheep sales, chained to pens or wheels or other convenient places.

The sheep-dog sees more of his master's ways than anybody. They start off together when the day is young, be the weather what it may. They are often companions in misfortune. Drenching rain, stinging hail, driving snow, or piercing wind may be their lot—it makes no difference. With bowed heads they plod along to do their duty among the waiting flock, and if we ever wake to a raging storm or a bitter winter gale, and think of some old hill shepherd and his dog, it is the steady, reliable, rough-haired bob-tail that seems the fit companion for the grizzled veteran with the crook.

On meeting one shepherd soon after shearing time I looked for his usual companion—a bob-tail with a very long shaggy coat, so matted together with mud that it would have defied any brush and comb. Instead of the mud-coated dog I saw a fresh one—a thin, gaunt creature, and I remarked: " You have a new dog, shepherd—what has happened to Bill ? " The shepherd smiled. " 'Tis still Bill ! " he said, " but he wur in such a pickle wi' mud in his coat that I sheared him ! I'd got the shears handy, you see, an' I said to him: ' I'm damned if I don't do you as well, Bill, now I be at it ! '

He beant hardly used to it yet, but he couldn't enjoy himself when the weather turned warm—still, come the winter, reckon he'll be the same ol' Bill again!'"

Among many pleasant memories of sheep-dogs and their owners I recall a meeting with John Beecher, a shepherd lad, in a valley east of Cissbury Ring. John was devoted to his work, and content to do it regardless of what future years might bring to members of his profession. With him were two rough-haired dogs, an old one and a young one which he was training. There was no water supply on the feeding-ground, so every day John took a large bottle of water with him, which was far more than he required, and after lunch he turned his empty waterproof dinner bag upside down, punched it in to form a bowl, and filled it with water for his shaggy friends.

I asked him to hold my staff and pose for a photograph so that I could use it as an illustration for this little record of his thoughtful action.

Collies used for sheep-dogs are often unsafe for strangers to handle, but Prince was an exception to the rule. When I met Shepherd Newell near the Devil's Dyke he had a fine collie for a companion. Newell's flock was usually penned for the dinner hour in an enclosure near the Dyke Hotel, consequently Prince found many friends. It was only natural that constant attentions from visitors made him "soft" from the shepherd's point of view, but his master, a dear, quiet old man, smiled indulgently when ladies exclaimed: " Oh, what a beautiful dog!" and fed him with dainties of all kinds. " He gets plenty of nice chocolates and things given to him," said Newell, " but the ladies don't think to say: ' Will shepherd have one?'"

I stayed in the enclosure while the shepherd had dinner, which was brought to him from his home, and Prince sat very close beside me on a bank. I shall never forget that meal. The pieces I gave him seemed so small and inadequate, and were gobbled so quickly, that I was almost ashamed to look into those beautiful eyes and note their wistful, pleading expression. Prince soon finished my lunch; his long soft nose went to the bottom of the bag and not a crumb was wasted. Then I whispered in his ear, and apologized to him for the shortage, as we sat cuddled up with our heads together, and he kissed me to show that he understood what I said. Call me silly if you like—but any dog lover would have done the same!

# THE ODD CHAPTER

THERE are some items in my note-books which are not important enough for a special chapter;—trivial records and quaint remarks gathered since the publication of former books. What is one to do with such oddments? They have no definite place, yet, because each of them is connected with shepherds or sheep or with some particular Sussex man, they claim their share of space in an Odd Chapter.

As an instance I have a note of a chat with a shepherd on the West Sussex Downs, who told me about the wonderful restoration to health of his daughter. She had been troubled with a tendency to consumption, but was cured by regular attendance at the sheep-fold each morning when the ewes were roused and driven over the hills. The strong odour from the sheep at this time has strange beneficial properties—a fact which is overlooked by many people who might be better for the same treatment.

Perhaps it is possible that constant work in this odour strengthens the shepherds. We do not find many of them weakened by colds and chest complaints. The old men I have known who were past work were mostly troubled by rheumatism, heart weakness, and giddiness, or rupture, all of which might be traced to exposure to weather or to strain through heavy work such as pitching, carrying, and shearing.

I was walking over the downs with a shepherd who had folded his flock and was on his way home. He pointed to some Round Headed Rampion flowers, and said: "They be pretty !—there be three kinds of this sort of flower, all much alike, as you might say, and one of them is my mother's favourite, but it beant this one, an' I haven't seen many this year—reckon 'tis too dry for 'em or somethin'." I guessed the plants he referred to and kept a sharp watch as we threaded our way between the many furze bushes. Presently I was lucky enough to find what I looked for—a small Scabious, and a Devil's Bit Scabious, both in bloom. Instantly he picked out the Devil's Bit as the favourite, and he carefully packed away each of the plants in his dinner-bag so that he could take them home and tell his mother their names.

As we passed a field of young corn at the end of the Down a corncrake was calling. It appeared for a moment at the edge of the path, but hid again at our approach. Presently it called after us, and the shepherd remarked: "Do you hear what he be tellin' us ? He keeps on a-sayin' ' 'tis goin' t' be wet,' ' 'tis goin' t' be wet,'—an' most times 'tis true, so don't stay long 'bout or mebbe you'll get wet jacket !" We parted at the cross-roads, and the rain came before I reached home !

Pleasant memories often follow the casual mention of some particular thing. As I wrote the last paragraph I was reminded of another corncrake and hours spent with another shepherd.

In the course of our ramble we heard the call of a corncrake quite near us, among some herbage and low bushes. I told my friend that although I had caught many glimpses of these birds at various times I had never seen one in flight. "Ye might see it now if Mike finds him," he replied, and he had scarcely spoken when the bird was flushed by the dog and flew over some brambles and stunted gorse, but not quickly enough for safety, for the big dog darted after it, leaped nimbly in the air, caught it deftly, and brought it to his master. The shepherd took it, but it died in his hand. "Reckon you diddun want see *that*," remarked my friend. "I knows you, you see; I knows you likes t' see un *fly*, an' not see 'un *die*—though a landrail be good eatin';—at least *I* like 'em ef they be cooked proper."

When I left the shepherd that day I wished to visit somebody else, and asked him to suggest a way across the Downs. He showed me a little-used path. "You goo on till you comes to a stile," he said, "then over it into a hollow—'tis like a pudden-basin when you gets down in—an' then out t'other end over 'nother stile. These ol' paths be very handy," he continued, "but you want to know 'em! Now afore you goo I'll show you 'nother ol' path." He led me to a big gate and pointed over a ploughed field. "That *was* it," he said, "but 'twas ploughed up, an' now nobody knows no different. *I* shouldn' goo now, you unnerstand, being shepherd where I be, but ef I lef' here, an' comed back anywhen for a doddle round, an' cared t'goo across, there bean't anyone as could stop me!"

Such scraps of knowledge, hidden in the heads of shepherds and other workers in the country-side, are of increasing value in these days, when pedestrians have been practically driven off the main roads.

I followed the shepherd's directions and climbed the stile, and was soon in the "pudden-basin." I have been to lambing-folds tucked away in cosy hollows between hills, but this was different. I had no idea that such a place existed. Nothing was seen but turf and sky. The big, round, deep hollow was a place for day-dreams, and I lingered there for some time. It was a strange experience to lie there and watch some rooks pass overhead, for the depths of the green bowl gave them an unusual effect. At last I climbed the second stile and followed the path according to the shepherd's directions.

My habit of tramping about the country-side and using old footpaths, combined with my interest in flints and many downland subjects, earned me a local reputation. I was apparently considered to be mixed up with all the societies interested in archæology and downland and footpath preservation, for while chatting with a man who was mending a sheep fence on a farm he mentioned a certain hill and said: " Now, take that hill. We allus thought it *all* belonged to Mus Blank. I don't know why, I suppose 'cos he never said it didn't!—anyway, we never took t'sheep up there. Well, one day it come to it as we foun' out t' truth when *your* lot come 'long!" The word "archæological" was apparently too much for him, for he continued: "They come doddlin' roun' t' hill, an' measurin' up, an' foun' out as t'top o' t'hill warn't hissen at all! Now, nobody wouldn' ever a-known it ef these 'ere Archipeligo blokes hadn't gone ferretin' roun' there." He stopped to watch a bird until it disappeared, then he remarked: " Yes, I reckon they be useful, knowledgeable blokes, an' I don' say nought agin 'em."

My fame as an "Archipeligo bloke" seemed to follow me round, and many shepherds put by various things for me. Bells and tackle, crooks and shears, " shepherds' crowns," flints and ox-shoes, thatching needles, lanterns, bows, and many other things were my reward for sincere interest in the men and their work.

Shepherds have very sharp eyes and find many odd things on the Downs. Among the treasures saved for me were four polished flint axes from different localities. The best one was found by Ted Nutley at Pangdean. Albe Gorringe, of Brown's Farm, West Blatchington, also surprised me with a "shepherd's crown" which he termed "a curiosity one"—a rare specimen, with the shell of the creature on it almost intact.

I have a store of such things, which a broker's man would despise, yet to me they are more than curios from downland farms, more than souvenirs of wonderful hours, for they link me with men whose never-failing kindness was a revelation.

In some unfrequented places shepherds are authorized to challenge strangers who appear to be trespassing in search of rabbits or game. I have accompanied a certain shepherd occasionally when he has left his dog in charge of the sheep and hurried after trespassers, and have enjoyed the fun. Once we had an exciting run after two poachers with dogs. Another time a man who was cornered stated that he was trying to get to the village. "I watched you come *from* there when I was top o' the hill," said the shepherd drily, "*so you diddun come here t' find it!* Now, if you beänt lookin' for trouble you bes' turn roun' an' goo straight back way you comed!" The man was a bronzed, tough-looking customer, but he went away at once as directed. "A bit of a rough un!" remarked my friend, "but I beänt feared of anyone while I got my crook in my hand." Then he smiled, and said: "He diddun expec' that, did he? I see quite a lot when I be up top o' that hill!"

In spite of doing such duties the shepherd was not supposed to take even a rabbit for his own use, but rabbit-pie happened to be one of his favourite dishes, so when his larder was nearly empty a quiet hour with his dog, on the way home, generally rewarded him to his satisfaction.

It is absurd to expect a man who is practically alone among downland hills and valleys, and whose reward for all his work is so small, to refrain from picking up a cheap dinner. Some men set snares as they go along, but this shepherd was like others who prefer to use their crook to obtain what is desired.

A sheep crook is not an easy tool to handle, but a shepherd is so used to it that the capture of a sheep appears quite simple to other people. The crook can be handled just as deftly to obtain a dinner, although the fact is not generally known. The spots where hares and rabbits rest are often noted. We see such places ourselves when the creatures rise suddenly at our approach and bolt away—cosy hollows pressed into shape by the crouching bodies. These spots are marked by the shepherd, and next time he is near he approaches quietly, with the crook-stick gripped firmly and the crook pointing downwards. The bed is often empty, but if the shepherd's keen eyes tell him that it is occupied the crook is swung, like a golf club, with such precision that the rabbit or hare is knocked on the head and killed instantly. A trap or snare is often cruel to the victim, but nothing could be less cruel then such skilful use of a sheep-crook as demonstrated to me on a Sussex hill.

When commenting on this fact the shepherd told me that he was with his sheep near the farm one day when the local blacksmith came to shoot a cow and paused to talk to two other men. He was about to walk across and join them when he noticed a hare crouching. He used his crook to get her, in his usual quiet way. He pocketed the hare, and thought his action unobserved, but later the blacksmith surprised him by saying: " That was a pretty smart piece of work, shepherd, when you got that hare ! "

Another tale had reference to a different animal, and he was moved to action by a different motive. As we stood talking a bunch of sheep were all gazing at some object in the herbage, which proved to be only crumpled paper. " They be like that," he remarked, " they stares at anythin' fresh, an' when they does it I likes t' know what 'tis, for once 'twas somethin' I didn't reckon to see." On that occasion the object of their interest proved to be an exhausted starving fox, with his front limbs lacerated by a snare. "He were a beautiful red fox!" said the shepherd, "an' 'twas sad to see him in such a state! I jus' swung me crook once, like I do to a rabbit or hare, an' put him out o' his misery."

From Jesse Moulding, the shepherd at Goring, I learned that his father and uncle (both shepherds) became experts in stone throwing. They practised so much that at last they could hit any desired object. A tobacco-box made a handy target, or if anyone cared to put a halfpenny on top of a stake they would prove their skill that way. The stone always hit the coin, which was generally lost. Rabbits were killed with one blow from a stone thrown at them. His uncle Jesse was particularly proficient, and with a stone was known to have killed a hare from a long distance.

Some of the excavations on prehistoric camping sites on Sussex hills have revealed pits filled with water-worn pebbles, presumably brought from the seashore. The fact causes one to wonder whether these smooth stones, suitable for throwing, were used in the way the brothers Moulding used theirs, for the purpose of procuring food.

Among the various shepherds' possessions which I have acquired for my collection is one that cannot be included in any usual list of shepherds' gear. This is a wooden bludgeon—a terrible weapon, with a large knob. It was apparently carved from a root, and has a hole through the end of the handle to hold a cord, by which, presumably, it was hung on the wrist ready for use. It belonged to shepherd John Norris, of Coate Farm, Durrington. Norris carried it when on the Downs after dark as a protection against any rough characters who might be about. The fact that such a thing was necessary is an index to the presence of undesirables in that lonely district in his time.

(A further reference to men bent on mischief, if nothing worse, has already been recorded in my interview with Charles Trigwell.)

A sheep-fold is such a common sight that one would scarcely expect to find anything to write about concerning the wattles used in its construction, but a shepherd, while pitching his fold, complained to me about the wattles provided for his use. These came from Crawley, and were made of chestnut wood, and although nearly new were already splitting and falling to pieces. " There be only one good wattle on this farm now," he said; " they was all sold, but one got covered with straw by the thatcher." Then he described the old oak wattles, which were made with cross-braces overlapping at the top and pegged to the slats, and told me that there were some stored in the Wattle House at Findon fair-ground. When I went to the fair I saw them in use, dividing some pens. There are many more of the same old type, but not so high, which are used for the fronts of the pens. These allow visitors to view the sheep easily. Old William Shepherd, who posed for his portrait beside a pen, told me that the low wattles were made expressly for this purpose. They offer an extra item of interest to those who like any little link with past days.

William Shepherd the shepherd has probably been photographed more than any other member of his profession in Sussex, and his portrait appears constantly in newspapers and magazines. Findon Fair and other gatherings bring him into the limelight, for every stranger slackens his or her pace to glance at " Old Shep." Dressed in a sort of thin white smock, a round black hat, and gaiters, he walks around and finds amuse-

*Photos by the Author*

1. A ROLLER-WATTLE
2. A SHEEP IN DISTRESS

WALTER WOOLER IN SMOCK

MICHAEL BLANN PLAYING WHISTLE-PIPE

*Photos by the Author*

ment as he may. His ancient crook is carried in his pocket, and is slipped on his stick when he is requested to pose before a camera.

William Shepherd was born at Duncton near Petworth on 31st December, 1846. "That's the day I was born," he said to me. "I don't say I remember it, but I was there, and so was my mother!"—by which you will understand that eighty-four years sat lightly on " Old Shep " that day. He works occasionally as a rabbit-catcher and mole-trapper, but having been a shepherd for fifty-seven years he still takes a keen interest in Findon and other sheep sales. Even a few minutes' chat with him on the fair ground is sufficient to make one wish to have him for a companion for a longer time, for it is probable that, given a quiet corner, his pipe, and a glass of good beer, he would gradually reveal a store of little items of passing interest. " But 'tis a job to get good beer now," he said. " Time was when you could get a glass o' beer wi' a good head o' froth on it. That showed that John Barleycorn was in it! There is no Barleycorn in modern beer. It is almost pizen ! " That is the verdict of " Old Shep."

Two odd items about sheep are worth a note here :

Those who visit lambing-folds in spring sometimes see a black lamb or two among the babies. These always provoke some comments, as they offer a fine contrast to the Southdowns and white Crossbreds and tempt us to take snapshots of them, but unfortunately their portraits are seldom entirely satisfactory. Even the best flocks are not free from these little black strangers. They are always an unwelcome surprise, and are drafted to the butcher as soon as possible.

We are all used to the sight of sheep with neatly trimmed short tails, but Mr. Arthur Beckett informed me that years ago, a flock of fat-tailed sheep were kept in a Sussex park, and were provided with little two-wheeled carriages to bear their heavy tails. An illustrated interview with the shepherd who tended such an unusual flock would have made an interesting addition to this book, but the mere record proves that a history of the shepherds of Sussex ought to have been written long ago.

Most of us have noticed starlings on the backs of sheep. They go there to search for ticks in the wool, consequently sheep and shepherd welcome their company. Less frequently jackdaws may be seen on sheep, and I have written of the habit of a magpie at Falmer which came to a fold each day to catch dor-beetles and took them on the backs of sheep to eat them. Wagtails are often seen among grazing sheep and in folds, and their appetite for flies ensures a welcome.

A pair of carrion crows at one lambing-fold provoked the shepherd. " Reckon I'll have t'get my gun out," he said. " I don't like they crows, an' t'sheep don' like 'em neither. 'Tis bein' short-handed you see. The fold wants tidyin' up, an' they crows knows it! They knows I had no chance to bury the cleanin's this mornin'. There be rather a lot o' muck lyin' 'bout, fur I had a busy night las' night."

This shepherd is singularly particular in his dislike of feminine visitors to his lambing-fold. Once he said to me: " Boss's wife be too fond o' pokin' 'bout here. If I got a ewe as wants a doctor I fastens t'wattle tight. I wunt have women lookin' on while *I* be doctor, fur tint decent!"

One of his experiences of lambing time is worth recording. He was working for a gentleman farmer, and had entire charge of the sheep, but at lambing time the owner came to look at the fold, and found him attending to a ewe that was ill and very weak. ('Twur a biggish place, an' he wur a real genelman, you unnerstand," explained the shepherd.) The farmer was very sorry for the ewe and said : " Can nothing be done for her, shepherd ? " and my friend replied : " Yes, 'twould be a great help to her if you could give her some gruel and a good dose of whisky in it." The boss smiled at such a request. He had never attended to sick sheep. " Well, John," he said, " if you really mean it she shall have it." " I certainly *do* mean it," replied old John, " though I s'pose you be thinkin' as *I* be arter a drop o' whisky, but I beant, an' if I had any I'd give it to t'ewe." Soon the boss departed and after an interval the shepherd was visited by a stately butler, who appeared with a tray, on which rested a large bowl of gruel and *two* tumblers of whisky !

There have been many references to an ancient custom of putting a lock of sheep-wool into the coffin of a shepherd. The wool was supposed to signify that the deceased was excused from attendance at church, owing to the fact that shepherds are compelled to work on Sundays. A specific instance relating to a Sussex man is noted in Miss Gossett's *Shepherds of Britain*.

A recent instance, with slight alteration, was recorded in the *Sussex County Herald* on 28th March, 1930, as follows :

" The funeral took place at Alfriston Church on Tuesday of Mr. Job Lamb, of High Street, Alfriston, who died on the previous Saturday, aged 72.

" Mr. Lamb, who had spent most of his life on the Downs with the sheep before his health compelled him to take lighter occupation two years ago, came to Alfriston 27 years ago from Ditchling, and he was well known at both places as one of the ' old Sussex shepherds.'

"As the coffin was being lowered, a piece of lamb's wool was dropped upon it. This is an old Sussex custom, and it was carried out by the desire of Dr. Evelyn English, his late employer."

In November, 1930, the *Southern Weekly News* recorded a quaint ceremony at a shepherd's funeral, when his crook and shears and a sheep-bell were buried with him :

"When Mr. Edward Duly, a Sussex shepherd, was buried at Falmer on Tuesday, his crook, shears, and a sheep-bell were interred with him.

"Mr. Duly, who was 58 years of age, died as he had lived, surrounded by his sheep. He was in the employ of Mr. N. E. Bannister, at Court Lodge Farm, Barcombe, and on Friday morning he apparently had a heart seizure while at work, and he was found dead among his flock. He had worked for Mr. Bannister for five years, and his employer speaks in the highest terms of praise of his work and devotion to his duty."

Commenting on the occurrence, another shepherd said to me : "I knew Duly when he was at Falmer. I've seen him sometimes standing near the sheep quiet like, and looking at nothing, as you might say. I thought 'twas a bit strange then, but now 't seems as if 'twas his heart made him do it ! "

During conversations with Sussex shepherds one may notice a peculiarity in their occasional use of the word "damn." It often has a meaning quite apart from the curse usually signified. It is used as an interjection—an exclamation expressing more than one mood. It may denote disgust or surprise. Here are some examples :

"I wouldn' a had *thet* said to *me* !—damn ! I'd ha' walked off quick and left un ! "

"First they diddun want I !—they wanted *'e*, an' they

*'ad 'e.* Then they *diddun* want *'e,* an' wanted *I* back. Damn!—I diddun goo! I said: '*You got 'e—you putt up wi' 'e!*'"

A man, relating an incident, said: "I seed summat in de pond, an' I says to myself 'Damn! I wonder what thet be then!'"

Another shepherd, who had promised me a knob from a bullock horn, looked for it in vain for some time. At last he discovered that he had it in use as a keyminder. He left it on the string till I went to see him, so that I should understand his delay in finding it. "Here 'tis," he said, "tied on this key—an' bin 'angin' there all that time! Damn! why, I picked un up mos' days, an' never noticed un! I couldn' help laughin' when I foun' un! Damn! I says: 'Here you be then! I'll jus' let ye bide till Mus Wills comes 'long, an' let him see ye!'"

Here are a few notes jotted down after conversations with shepherds:

The following incident was related quite seriously by one old man, who was showing me his pocket-knife. "I had another knife, too," he said, "when I was only seventy-six, but I gave it to an old man I was working with. He hadn't nara knife to cut up his dinner, and I couldn't bear to see him picking at his meat! He couldn't give me anything for the knife, and that worried him a bit, so I said: 'Look now—you be eighty-four and I be only seventy-six. If you give me four of your years, and call yourself eighty, I'll put 'em on my seventy-six and be eighty, and we'll both be level!' So he agreed, and we did it, but after dinner, as we was digging out a ditch by the side of the road, a man came doddling along, and stopped to watch us. All of a sudden he said to me: 'You be two pretty old buffers to be doing work like that!—how old might you be?' So I answered: 'We be a hundred and sixty, sir—we be eighty each!'

'I shouldn't have thought it,' he said—'your friend looks much older than you do.' So then I had to own up that I was quite young—only seventy-six—and told him all about it."

It may seem strange for a man to think himself "quite young" at seventy-six, but when he told me the tale he was nearly ninety.

---

A shepherd amused me with an account of some blackberry pickers. "They berry-pickers be a noosance, times," he said. "I mind one day there was some as comed too near t' sheep fur my likin', all rampagin' 'bout an' shoutin'. So I crep' up behin' t' thick booshes, an' med a noise like a bull. Then I shouts: 'Look out, Jim!—head 'un off if 'e breaks thro' thet side,' an' I rustles t' booshes wi' t' crook-stick. Diddun they jes run! Lord! they went like flies, an' I wur soon quiet agen!"

---

I have a note of a remark made by the same man in sly reference to a visitor who had given us his opinions about dogs rather freely. We doubted what he said, and when he had gone I said: "Shepherd—why didn't you correct him? You are an expert on dogs!" "Well," he replied, "there be some as *knows*, an' some as on'y *thinks* they knows, an' when a man as knows meets one o' t'otheruns 'e shuts up like a trap. If I'd told 'im what I thought of 'im 'e might not 'a' liked it!"

---

Another old man, while chatting to me, remarked: "I don't know what *you* think of the times, but *I* don't like 'em! There ain't nothen, hardly, same as 'twas!

We haves leather that ain't leather at all, an' jam that ain't jam, an' lots more that *I* never thought to see. Now-days you wants good eyesight to find a boy or girl what's innocent, an' good-mannered. The way they grows up they knows what they shouldn't know, an' they don't know what they ought to! They knows their way to the 'picture-palace' soon as they can walk in the street; but other things!—why! there be plenty runnin' 'bout as don't know a swede from a turnip!"

---

My friend N—— is a very peaceful man. I did not know that he had strong views about show flocks until I mentioned them. "They beant in *my* line," he said. "I wur brought up as a hill shepherd. I couldn' stand a show flock. I ha'n't forgot when my sheep was put 'tween two pens o' they show sheep at a sale. One o' the men wi' 'em looked at my lot an' said: 'Ha'en't ye got nara a pair o' shears, then, shepherd?' I diddun like that much, an' I said: 'Beant it bad 'nough to be putt here 'tween you two wi'out talkin' 'bout it?' Their sheep was nicely turned out an' their feet were very clean, so presently I says: 'Don't you *ever* take your sheep for a walk, then?—I see they've all got clean shoes on!' 'No,' he says, 'not often, an' allus very careful like—not racin' 'bout same as yours goos on!' So then I says: '*I* be a hill shepherd! I wouldn' be any good to look after tame rabbits!'"

---

It is so unusual to hear one shepherd complain of another that I made a note of the following comment of one man. Speaking about bells, he said: "My noo mate has a canister or two. I'll ask him 'bout 'em somewhen, but 'e is a hard man to talk to. Why! most days it 'ud upset him if you on'y tickled his back wi' a feather!

You can't get nara smile out of him. I do jus' hate to see anyone so damn miserable!"

---

Old Shepherd C—— was a jolly old man, although he was "in his eighty-one," and often ill. His wife was also merry and bright, but sometimes she appeared to be dismayed at his free-and-easy way with people. Once, when I knocked at their door, C—— opened it. "Hullo!" he said, "you come pokin' round here again? Come in an' shut t' door, an' we can have a chat." A voice from the kitchen interrupted. "That's a nice way to talk to a gentleman, Charlie, when he comes to see you!" "Well," bawled the shepherd in return, "I *be* pleased to see him, if he *have* come pokin' round. *I asked him to come in!* I wouldn't ask him in if I wa'n't pleased to see him!"

Even in serious moments his expressions were quaint. A certain man whom he expected had not arrived. "An' a good job, too," he remarked. "He likes a drop o' beer, but he lifts his elbow too many times. I'm glad 'twas you came instead. I do like a chat, but I can't abide talkin' to a fool!"

I had a many a laugh that afternoon, and when I left the old man bubbled over again. "Good-bye, good-bye. I'll see you at the Assizes," he said, and because his wife was listening he winked and added: "Come in when you're pokin' round here again!"

---

Nelson Coppard, his son-in-law, and his grandson were at work in the lambing-fold when I arrived, and a tiny grandson (the youngest member of the family) was there with a sheep-dog puppy. These two babies were investigating everything and learning many things for the first time. After inspecting the pens the shepherd suddenly told me that he had a good idea for a picture for this book, so I unpacked my camera. He made the child hold the crook and told him to keep steady, and gave him the pup on a chain. Grandfather's commanding manner awed both the boy and the puppy, and both stopped still and looked at us. "Now, if you can get that proper 'twould make a good picture," said the shepherd, an' you could call it : ' Break 'em in young.' " I liked his idea. I did my part quickly and quietly, and the result is seen in the next illustration.

## The Roller-wattle

In Gilbert White's *Natural History of Selborne* is the following note :

> "The sheep on the Downs this winter (1769) are very ragged, and their coats much torn; the shepherds say that they tear their fleeces with their own mouths and horns, and they are always in that way in mild, wet winters, being teased and tickled with a kind of lice."

As the only other reference to horned sheep relates to flocks then in West Sussex it may be that these were the sheep that were so teased and tickled.

The roller-wattle was designed to give momentary relief to sheep troubled with ticks. It is one of those odd things that are seldom noticed, yet it deserves attention, for it is a sign of somebody's thought for the sheep's comfort. The illustration is from a photograph taken at Patching. The roller, between two uprights, is set at a convenient height, so that the sheep may walk under it and rub themselves by moving to and fro. Fat ewes that roll over are sometimes unable to rise, and soon die unless assistance is given. The roller-wattle saves many sheep from using the ground, and although one man assured me that he had once seen a sheep on its back beside a roller I am tempted to think that it may have slipped while rubbing its back.

The second illustration shows a ewe on her back (and a roller in the background!). She was soon turned over, but was allowed to lie a moment longer than she might have done in order that I could obtain a picture of her.

As lambing time approaches the shepherd is constantly watching his heavy ewes in case one rolls over, but anyone who finds a sheep upside down should set it on its feet immediately, or obtain help.

On some farms where no roller-wattle is provided shepherds carry out the idea by erecting a "rubbing rail"—two pairs of sticks, each pair driven in the ground in the form of an X, hold a pole which is tied on the supports.

The shepherd's remarks quoted by Gilbert White apparently prove that roller-wattles and rubbing-rails were unknown in 1769.

I was once trying to obtain a roller-wattle for a museum, so while chatting with an old shepherd, as he trimmed some lambs, I led up to the subject, but he said: "T'ent mine, or you should have it. 'Tis t' boss's roller, but I 'spect he'll arrange it if you speak. 'Tis time us had a new 'un anyway!" Off I went to the farmer—a kind, jovial man, who had given me things before, and who treated my study of sheep-bells, flints, shepherds, and their gear with tolerance and quiet amusement. I was surprised that even an offer of a pound for the ancient article was instantly refused. He said: "I'm not going to part with it!" and I knew that any further argument would be a waste of breath.

I went back to the shepherd. "Well," he said, "did you get un?" I shook my head, and explained that the boss refused to part with it, even for a pound. "Then he's a fool!" burst out the old man impetuously—"why, damme, he only gave two shillin' for un, an' that I *do* know! Damn! why, it do mek me wild for any man t' be such a fool, even if he be rich an' be in orkard mood!" The shepherd looked very straight at me, then he remarked: "'Tis on'y a fool turns away good money. *I* never turn away money—'tis hard to get 'nough!" I realized that this was my opportunity. He had always been very busy when I had met him, and now I said: "Shepherd! I'll take you at your word. Will you leave your work for once and pose for a photograph for a shilling?" "Reckon I will!" he replied, briskly. "I'd do *anythin'* for a shillin'!" He stopped work, arranged a lamb in the bows and stood as I told him. He was a perfect model: the light was good, and the result was the best photograph ever obtained of this old Sussex shepherd.

### Shepherds' Sundials

The shepherds of to-day usually carry a reliable watch, and I have already recorded how one man, whose favourite watch could not be repaired, carried a small kitchen clock in a bundle of cloth in a hare pocket. Although I had read of dials cut in the turf in past days, I scarcely hoped to track down much information concerning them, but when Nelson Coppard told me about his life as shepherd boy, and mentioned a dial cut in the turf for his use at Horton by Michael Blann, I followed the clue eagerly. At a later date Mr. Blann willingly gave me the details of dials which he made.

He had no watch at that time (about sixty years ago), and could not afford to buy one, but he owned a little pocket compass, which he used in arranging the dials. It was quite a business to make this type of clock. His method was to select a flat place where the turf was short, and draw a circle about eighteen inches in diameter. A hole was made in the centre to hold the end of his crook stick. The stick was held perfectly upright, and where it threw its shadow at each hour cuts were made and turf removed—a narrow cut near the stick and widening a little towards the edge of the clock. Sometimes he walked a long way to be on the spot to mark a shadow line correctly at the hour. "I had two or three of those clocks," he said, "so that wherever I was I knew the time, if 'twas sunny." On approaching a "clock" he stood the crook stick in the hole, perfectly upright, and noted the time. He did not leave a permanent stick there, as it might have drawn attention to the spot. Sometimes the sheep fed over the clock, but if necessary he kept the turf clipped short for his own convenience.

While chatting to George Humphrey at Findon Fair I happened to mention the matter to him, and gathered further information. "Sundials?" he said. "Yes, my father made one for me at Selsey, but not a turf one. He made it of clay brought from a distance, and arranged it on a bank. It was just like a clock face and he made it by using his watch and marking on the clay." This dial not only had hour marks, but a mark for every quarter of an hour, and George used it constantly. The gnomon was not a stick, but a big nail. From this, rows of dots, pricked with the point of a nail, radiated to each division of the outer edge. The sun baked the clay hard, and the clock lasted well. Later his father improved on the dial by constructing a carefully finished one of the same kind in a cheese box and drying it well. This could be carried to any place where they were working, and having been placed in position correctly could be left and used until they moved to fresh ground.

"My father was always busy," said Mr. Humphrey; "he did all kinds of things on winter evenings. He made us clay marbles and baked them in the oven.

He made rush seats for chairs, too. We made our own candles then. We had the moulds and things for doing it, and work like that passed away the dark hours."

### Shepherds' Shelters

In the chapter " The First Shepherds of Sussex " will be found a reference to rough " huts " or shelters used by some shepherds living in a state of civilization similar to those of prehistoric times.

It is worthy of note that this custom has lingered until recent years, for we have evidence that Sussex shepherds of the eighteenth and nineteenth centuries made rude shelters for their occasional comfort. These were natural hollows in banks roofed over, or convenient holes enlarged and finished off, and lined with dry straw, heath, fern, or other material gathered for the purpose.

In *Contributions to Literature*, by M. A. Lower (1854), the author quotes the following words of an old shepherd who died previous to that date :

"The life of a shepherd in my young days was not the same as it is now. You very seldom see a shepherd's hut on our hills in these times, but formerly every shepherd had one. Sometimes it was a sort of cave dug in the side of a bank or link, and had large stones inside. It was commonly lined with heath or straw. The part above ground was covered with sods of turf or heath or straw or boughs of hawth. In rough, shruckish weather the shepherd used to turn into his hut and lie by the hour together, only looking out once in a while to see that the sheep didn't stray away too far. Here he was safe and dry, however the storm might blow overhead, and he could sit and amuse himself as he liked best."

My interview with shepherd George Humphrey records how he made himself a shelter in a rabbit bury and also a "shepherd's bush."

## Shepherds' Music

The enthusiast who endeavours to secure records in one particular county is apt to find the task far more difficult than collecting information about one subject from all sources. For instance, although there are references to shepherds playing whistle-pipes and other musical instruments in past days, yet to find a Sussex shepherd who has actually done so is unusual. It is only by diligent enquiry, or by luck, that such men are discovered.

I knew that jews'-harps were often used, and George Humphrey remembered hearing shepherd boys playing their whistles to the sheep. Later, while chatting to Albert Aucock of Wilmington he told me that in his young days a friend of his, a shepherd boy named Fred Parsons, played a whistle-pipe. At Alfriston I found Mr. Parsons (then aged 72). Although he did not remain a shepherd he remembered his days as shepherd boy, about 1870. He used to take his whistle-pipe with him while minding sheep, and also used an accordion. The latter was generally hidden on the hills. "I used to cut out a big turf and hide the accordion under it," he said, "then it was where I wanted it." "Flocks were larger then," he remarked. "Where I tended we had a thousand sheep." He also told me that while on the hills he carved out figures, crosses, and other objects in chalk. Sometimes he brought them home, but sixty-odd years had passed since then, and figures, whistle-pipe and accordion had disappeared, and only pleasant memories remained. "I had many a tune on those old hills," he said, as he pointed to them.

At last I met Michael Blann, an old shepherd, who lived till he was ninety. As recorded in my account of him on another page, I found that he still had a treasured whistle-pipe which he once used on the hills. The accompanying portrait shows him playing a tune for my benefit. The other photo shows the whistle-pipe, with his precious song book in which he wrote the words of his favourite old songs. Thus my search ended with a wonderful find.

Many incidents in the lives of the old shepherds on Sussex hills can be truthfully reconstructed from this book of records. Among them we can picture a peaceful scene of a flock of tegs quietly feeding while the shepherd boy passes the time playing to them on his whistle-pipe.

## SHEPHERDS OF THE MARSHES

MY interest in the shepherds of the marshes began when I acquired a large sheep-hook from Kent. I was collecting material for my history of the shepherds of Sussex, and was anxious to know whether such hooks were also used in the county, but as numerous enquiries failed to bring any information I went to Rye to investigate. By a lucky chance I stayed at the Olde Bell Inn and found that my host, Mr. Fletcher, was able to give me an introduction to a shepherd. Thus the way was paved for my entry into a new and fascinating world.

After years among the downland shepherds my visit to those of the south-east corner of the county proved a great surprise. I found the sheep, feeding-grounds, methods, and crooks all different. Even the familiar word "shepherd" was not heard, for in this district shepherds are known as "lookers." Only one thing was exactly the same, and that was the courtesy and unexpected kindness shown by men and their families whose lives are spent among flocks. My welcome compensated me for the journey and for the necessary tramping which is the lot of the rambler in a land where dikes take the place of hedges and fences.

The Sussex marshes around Rye and Winchelsea extend to the Kent Ditch, which is the county boundary. Fields, flat and green, divided by dikes and tenanted by flocks, stretch for miles. The sheep are of a sturdy, hardy kind, known as the "Kent," or "Romney Marsh"

Song

1

It is a dirge of a poor tar
Like that well done

I am a jolly fellow
And a jolly tar I
Sometimes like some of the ts
The ocean is always my
My worth go round
To me'tis right ——
Well no one su.... ——
But sail sing and work
From morn till night our
And then I will drink my
Town
I like a dirge of a good tar too
Since forget of a drop of ——
Let gentlemen fine top down ——
And will stick to my beer.

2

Thus idly, that my Wife
Like that well alone
One woman happy in life
A woman on the name of the
She must be some ... the ...
Is grasping ...  ...
Her ever, after a very light
Like me she wants her tea.

3

Others is my dirge of tea
He thinks he ... well ... Rythm
We work on to ... we are despise him
He sits lazy upon an easy
Though old in age but pretty ...
He has not found her there is
Boys if you leave tea't need gold
But till to will stick to tea

*Photo by the Author*

TIM GODDEN AND "TURK" OF WINCHELSEA

breed, and the lambs, which arrive later than baby Southdowns, are very attractive. The flocks roam about on their allotted spaces, and need little other food than grass, as the pastures are very rich.

There is no need for a shepherd of the downland type to lead the sheep about all day. The looker makes his daily round knowing that his charges are where he put them—in the "fourteen acres," or the "twenty acres," and so on, which is the local way of referring to each field. An enquiry for a man may bring the reply: "You'll find him in the fourteen acres." Sometimes a zig-zag course is necessary to reach the looker in a distant field. There are no short cuts. You must cross the dikes by the proper route, by double gates, or planks, or by quaint little bridges, and at every crossing there is something to attract one's attention and compel one to linger.

Unlike the shepherds on the downs, lookers do not carry crooks. They have big iron "lambing-hooks" for catching lambs and sheep by the neck, but these are only in general use at lambing time, which begins in April.

These hooks are mounted on long stick handles which usually measure about eight feet. The illustration shows a specimen (without the stick) the outline of which would touch the margins of a paper 14 inches by 10 inches. The hooks are made at local forges, but, naturally, orders are infrequent, as the hooks last so long. The proper span of the opening to the crook head is reckoned to be a width which allows the first, second, and third fingers, held together in line, to slide through comfortably.

At Castle Farm, near Winchelsea, I found Mr. Tom Godden, the head looker, who has been among sheep all his life. He started as a "tar-boy" and now has charge of flocks roaming over about a thousand acres. It was his custom, until deafness and ailments altered his daily routine, to make his round of inspection on horseback, and interview the lookers working under him.

Very little schooling was considered necessary when Tom Godden was a boy. He went with other scholars to an old dame at Guldeford. The recollection of those days amused him when he told me about them, and he said: "I don't think she could read or write properly herself, but she taught us to draw big capital letters and figures."

My first visit was on a dull day, and my photographs were not very good, but on my second visit I obtained a picture of Tom Godden with his favourite dog. He is holding a lambing-hook which he has had for over fifty years, and which belonged to his father. In his early days he liked to keep his hook as bright as silver.

To my great delight I received the old hook for my shepherds' museum, a welcome souvenir of my visit to Castle Farm.

It was fortunate for me that I stopped for a chat with a man who was resting by the roadside after using a swap-hook. "If you want to know anything about the marshes or sheep," he said, "you should find Ernest Wratten at East Guldeford," so to East Guldeford I went, and in due course found Mr. Wratten, who proved a good friend. He has sheep on the marshes and is an enthusiastic naturalist, with a wonderful knowledge of the birds of the locality, so we found that we had much in common. His interest in my book was proved by an introduction to a looker of the same unusual name (Tom Wratten), a supply of useful details, and a gift of an old lambing-hook used by his father, who spent fifty years "lookering" in one place.

While we watched his little daughter feeding two "bottle babies," I asked him about the use of sheep-bells, as I had not heard any during my ramble. He said that it is very unusual to hear one. There is no necessity to use them, although he can remember occasional instances years ago. Even then a single bell was considered sufficient, and "rings" or sets of bells are not known.

Mr. Wratten told me of a strange experience among the sheep. During a severe snowstorm, in which many animals were lost, one sheep was covered by a drift while in a deep corner on sloping ground. Three weeks afterwards the dog stopped to inspect a small hole in the hard drifted snow, and this led to the rescue of the sheep. Although covered by the drift it had managed to move about in the small hollow and to eat some grass, but it could not break through the white roof piled above it.

Near Mr. Wratten's house is a sheep-pen and a well-built "tun" or dipping-pool. Here sheep are dipped in accordance with the official regulation, and they are still washed before shearing.

While speaking of shearing (which is now done by machine) Mr. Wratten recalled the days of the shearing gangs fifty years ago, when he was eleven years old. Shearers were supplied with a cask of beer, and at a signal sound (a word which he can say but not spell) the men prepared to stop work. Sheep partly done had their legs strapped for the short interval. The boy then called "cock-up!" and the men stood upright, and beer was taken to them in turn in two tin mugs. Then shearing was resumed.

He also told me of another old custom. At the end of the shearing the shearers indulged in what they termed a "feast" of rum and sugar. He remembers that well, as it was his duty to fetch the rum from Rye. The rum was dropped on lumps of sugar, and sucked away, and Mr. Wratten states that "there was no rum wasted."

Another item worth recording was mentioned, namely, the old custom of planting an elder tree at every sheep-pen situated on the marsh away from the farms. It was used for sheep that had been attacked by flies. The leaves of the tree were bruised and rubbed on the sheep and the smell kept away the fly for a time. Other preparations are now in use, but some of the old trees are still standing.

My lambing-hooks are probably two of the oldest on the marshes. They link me to bygone days when their first owners had them new from the forge. They link me also to the men who gave them to me. When I handle them they bring me pictures of green acres and newly sheared sheep, of the lookers, of bird-haunted dikes, of reeds, bullrushes, water plaintains, and marsh mallows, and a hundred other things, but I treasure them particularly as reminders of remarkable unfailing kindness shown to me while rambling on the Sussex marshes.

## SUSSEX SHEEP

THE small proportion of facts and large proportion of fancy regarding the first shepherds of Sussex, with which we are obliged to be satisfied, applies equally to the first sheep. Even the fact that horned sheep existed here in prehistoric times is only known through chance discovery of skull remains, although horns were probably so useful that the scarcity of such evidence is accounted for. Sheep skins, also, must have been very valuable to Neolithic men, and many of the flint knives and scrapers found on their camping sites in Sussex were doubtless used in the work of skinning and preparing the hides of domestic animals and others.

I had found great enjoyment in the company of shepherds and much romance in the history of their lives, but it was a shock to realize that my knowledge of sheep was far less then my knowledge of the men who tend them, and because sheep and shepherds are inseparable I sought for more information.

From a friend who had endeavoured to collect some details about sheep in past days, I learned that the small number of important references in print disappointed him, but fortune favoured me when I wrote to the Southdown Sheep Society at Chichester. My visit to their office proved a delightful surprise. Figures and statistics are not sufficient for Mr. W. O. Stride and Mr. W. P. Ballantine. They are enthusiasts who keep a store of notes of all kinds relating to sheep, gathered from many sources, supplemented by pictorial records which link the daily work of the Society with the days of the first Southdown flocks. All their records were offered to me for my use, including a book, published by the advertising committee, entitled *The Southdown Sheep*, compiled by Mr. E. Walford Lloyd, a recognized authority on the subject. (As agricultural editor and correspondent, Mr. Walford Lloyd has probably written most of what there is to write on the sheep of the county, namely, the Southdown breed).

The opening paragraphs awaken interest in the subject in the most casual reader, and quotations from Arthur Young's *Annals of Agriculture* carry the reader along through the histories of Ellman and other noted breeders to the present Southdown show flocks. A valuable addition is a special chapter, entitled: "Round the Year with a Hill-flock," in which Mr. Walford Lloyd gives details of the hill-shepherd's duties throughout the year.

Without such a book one could hardly realize how the loving care from generations of flock masters and shepherds has transformed the old heath breed into the familiar Southdown of the present day, but after reading the following extracts a little imagination enables us to form pictures in the mind of the gradual changes in shepherds and flocks.

FROM

"THE SOUTHDOWN SHEEP"

*Compiled by E. WALFORD LLOYD*

Although the Southdown is undoubtedly the oldest of the Down breeds of sheep in the United Kingdom, its early history is more or less wrapped in a veil of mystery, but through this veil appears one undeniable fact, that upon those chalky hills from which the Southdown takes its name, an active, short-woolled breed of sheep flourished from time immemorial.

These sheep were certainly not Southdowns as we know them to-day, but these ancestors of the breed were grazing the short, sweet herbage of the Downs, without a doubt, when William the Norman set foot on English soil at Pevensey.

A connecting link with the old-time breed would appear to be given by the Rev. Gilbert White, M.A., who, writing in 1773, in *The Natural History and Antiquities of Selborne*, on Sussex, says:

"One thing is very remarkable as to sheep: from Westward till you get to the River Adur, all the flocks have horns, and smooth, white faces, and white legs, and a hornless sheep is rarely to be seen, but as soon as you pass that river Eastward, and mount Beeding Hill, all the flocks at once become hornless, or as they call them 'poll sheep'; and have, moreover, black faces with a white tuft of wool on their foreheads, and speckled and spotted legs, so that you would think that the flocks of Laban were pasturing on one side of the stream, and the variegated breed of his son-in-law, Jacob, were cantoned on the other. And this diversity holds good respectively on each side from the valley of Bramber and Beeding to the Eastward, and Westward the whole length of the Downs.

"If you talk with the shepherds on this subject, they will tell you that the case has been so from time immemorial, and smile at your simplicity if you ask them whether the situation of these two different breeds might not be reversed.

"However, an intelligent friend of mine, near Chichester, is determined to try the experiment, and has this autumn, at the hazard of being laughed at, introduced a parcel of black-faced, hornless rams among his horned Western ewes.

"The black-poll sheep have the shortest legs and the finest wool."

## JOHN ELLMAN

It was upon this speckled-legged heath breed that the great Master Breeder and "Father" of the present-day Southdown, Mr. John Ellman, of Glynde, built, when he took the improvement of the breed in hand and commenced a work which has triumphantly stood the test of the succeeding centuries.

John Ellman, the son of Richard and Elizabeth Ellman, was born at Hartfield, near East Grinstead, on 17th October, 1753, so Mr. F. P. Walesby tells us in that excellent Memoir on the great breeder, which appears in Baxter's Library of Agriculture.

His father, Richard, occupied a farm in the parish of Hartfield, at the time of his son's birth, and continued in it until 1761, when he removed to Glynde, near Lewes, where he died in 1780.

John Ellman was twice married, the first time in 1783, at Hartfield, to Elizabeth Spencer, whose son John was born in 1787, and who succeeded his father in the farm at Glynde, which he occupied for many years, and from which he removed to Landport, near Lewes.

In 1794, Mr. Ellman married for the second time, the lady being Constantia, daughter of the Rev. T. Davis, Vicar of Glynde.

The history of John Ellman is, practically, a history of the Southdown sheep, and so we make no apology for quoting largely from the works of the great Arthur Young, who, in his *Annals of Agriculture*, has left so vivid a picture of Ellman and the Southdown sheep, in his account of his tour through Sussex.

Writing of his visit to that county, and to John Ellman in 1788, or some ten years after this great breeder had started to improve the breed, Arthur Young says:

"The principal feature of the farms is sheep, the lands being exceedingly well adapted to them, for everyone has a share of the Downs, which seem here to the eye to rise on every side.

"Between Bourne and Steyning, which is 33 miles, the Downs are about six miles wide, and in this tract there are, it is said, about 200,000 ewes kept."

"I am inclined to think," says Arthur Young, "that this is (the soil considered) the highest stocking that is known in this kingdom, and ought to give us a good opinion of the breed, whatever it might be, that can be kept in such numbers on a given space of country.

"In the parish of Glynde, 900 acres have 1000 sheep, Mr. Morris has one ewe per acre in winter, and two and one-third per acre in summer, and another farm of 2000 acres had 3000 in summer, and 1500 in winter."

Then Arthur Young goes on to say:

"The best flocks I viewed were Miss Hayes', Mr. Ellman's, and Lord Sheffield's (speaking of the pure Southdowns, for his Lordship has other crosses).

"The true Southdowns when very well bred have the following points: No horns, a long speckled face, clean, thin jaw, a long but not thin neck, no tuft of wool on the forehead, which they call owl headed, nor any frize of wool on the cheeks. Thick in the shoulder, open breasted and deep, both fore and hind legs stand wide, round and straight in the barrel, wide upon the loin and hips, shut well in the twist, which is a projection of flesh on the inner part of the thigh, that gives a fullness when viewed behind, and makes a Southdown leg of mutton remarkably round and short, more so than in most other breeds. A thin speckled leg and free from wool, the belly full of wool, the wool close and hard to the feel, curdled to the eye and free from spiry projecting or staring fibres.

"It is an observation with which experienced sheep

masters in most countries will agree that a flat back without a ridge, a broad loin and thick carcase, with a close, hard wool coat, will stand the vissitudes of bad weather and hard food much better than a thin carcase, a narrow loin, and an open loose-woolled coat.

"Sheep that are well formed in these respects will at a pinching season be in better order than those that are thus worse made.

"In all respects the Southdown is an unexceptional breed, and this is proved beyond all doubt, from the fact that farmers keep them at the rate of 1½ to the acre. With regard to heavy stocking, Mr. Ellman, on 580 acres, has 700 ewes, rams, and wethers in winter, and 1450 of all sorts in summer, besides 140 head of cattle.

"Mr. Ellman's is a capital flock, and larger than the mean weight, but Miss Hayes' sheep are larger than his."

So great was the fame of the Southdowns at this time, and especially Mr. Ellman's flock, that we find them being sent to all parts of the country.

Thus, in the *Agricultural Annual* of 1836, we read:

"The first Southdown ram that was ever sold for ten guineas was sold in the year 1787, to Lord Waldegrave, in Essex, by Mr. Ellman, when he sold two to his Lordship for £21. The year previous, the celebrated Arthur Young bought 80 ewes of Mr. Ellman, at 18s., which were sent into Suffolk."

Messrs. Ramsden (Notts), Boys (East Kent), Macro and Crow (Norfolk) were also purchasers from this flock round about this time.

Four years later, the great "Coke, of Holkham,"

began to take an interest in the breed, through Mr. Ellman, who, having visited Holkham, suggested to Mr. Coke that he should try Southdowns, and on his return to Glynde, Ellman sent 500 ewes and lambs from the best flocks to Holkham, with four rams of his own.

In the memoir of Ellman, in Baxter's Library, appears a very good story concerning Glynde mutton and its delicate flavour.

> "When the (then) present Duke of Bedford was Lord Lieutenant of Ireland, he was once, when dining with Lord Sligo, earnestly recommended to taste a fine haunch of Glynde mutton, to which His Grace, himself a breeder and admirer of Southdowns, and well acquainted with Mr. Ellman, readily acceded, but no politeness to his noble host could induce him to finish the slice, or to say it was otherwise than rank in flavour, and terribly tough!
>
> "On enquiry, the disappointed Marquis ascertained that his shepherd, who had been ordered to kill the 'best' Southdown sheep, had actually slaughtered a ram for which Lord Sligo, a few weeks before, paid Mr. Ellman 200 guineas."

Writing on Ellman's flock in his *Annals of Agriculture*, Arthur Young speaks of Southdown wool thus:

> "Mr. Ellman's fleeces are the heaviest on the Downs, and yet he gets the highest price. That increasing quantity does not of necessity hurt the quality appears, Mr. Ellman remarked, from the wool staplers giving as much for that of fat wethers as of lean sheep; it must however be allowed that they assert it is not intrinsically worth so much, because when sorted it cannot be made so equal. Yet they

agree that it works better in the mill. Folding on chalky lands, they say, makes the wool harsh and not mill well, not being so soft and silky as the other, but the colour of it is very fine. The observation that the lighter the fleeces the better the wool, probably holds good when no particular care or attention is paid to the breed. Towards East Bourne, they run 20 or 21 to the tod, and their wool is reckoned in general the best of the Downs, but their sheep do not feed so well. Mr. Ellman has a practice which he thinks answers, that is to clip off the coarsest of the wool on the thigh and the dock a month before shearing, which he sells as locks at $3\frac{1}{2}$d. a lb., and the quantity is about 4 oz. per sheep, so it keeps them clean and cool in the hot weather. Another observation Mr. Ellman has made is that when sheep are well fed till Christmas, and afterwards hard kept, but got up again in flesh before shearing, which is a common case, it will be very perceivable in the wool. There will be a knot in the staple of it which, in working, will prove brittle and harsh, and lessen the value considerably."

We cannot refrain from once more quoting Arthur Young in the management of Ellman's flock. Writing in the *Annals*, this great authority says:

" The flock consists of 500 breeding ewes of three ages, each ewe produces three lambs, or more if twins, lambing at two, three, and four years old, and when they are four-and-a-half years old he sells them off to other flocks. The general practice has been to sell them to the graziers in the Weald of Sussex and Kent, who fatten both the ewe and the lamb the succeeding summer. He usually saves for store, 220 ewe lambs, which gives him an opportunity to refuse about 51 each of the several years. The ewe lambs are sent to keep on the Weald of Sussex, among the small farmers, until the succeeding Lady Day, when they are taken home and flocked, that is to say, they are folded of a night till a year and a half old, when they are mixed with the breeding ewes. He always takes 60 of his best ewes from the flock, which he puts to his best ram, and takes good care to save the rams from them. The usual mode is to allot 50 ewes to each ram, and to turn into the flock all the rams at the same time, but Mr. Ellman condemns this habit, and after he has taken out 60 ewes he puts three of his best rams remaining to his flock, and about five or six days afterwards, a couple more, and continues adding two every four or five days, till the whole are put in. He turns the rams into the flock about the 24th or 25th of October, and he lets them continue with the ewes about five weeks from first to last.

"Having but a small portion of down and sheep walk and his enclosed land being very wet, so that he cannot stock with store sheep, Mr. Ellman is obliged to depend on artificial food, turnips and hay during winter, rye grass, clover, and rye in spring, and tares and rape in summer. In giving his sheep turnips, he adopts the excellent practice of drawing them out of the ground three or four days before the sheep are put to them. By this good management, which ought to be more universally disseminated, they are not so likely to burst, which sometimes is the case if not drawn. He always gives the flock hay, or some dry food, to counteract the water in the turnips. If the turnips are not destroyed by frost, the ewes live on them from Michaelmas to Lady Day. The ewes are usually folded of a night throughout the year, except about a month or five weeks after lambing. The lambs are weaned about 12 or 14 weeks old.

> "The quality of Southdown wool is most certainly to be attributed in a great measure to the extremely short and sweet grass which grows on the hills, when the sheep are turned into artificial food or rich pasture it tends to throw out a more luxuriant fleece."

In connection with this dictum, it is the short, sweet grass of the Downland which gives Southdown mutton so succulent a taste, and of this Edmund Scott, writing in 1798, says:

> "The South Downs, in agricultural language, is a body of hill and vale in the county of Sussex, extending from Eastbourne, East to Shoreham River, West, they afford support to nearly 150,000 sheep, from which nearly 100,000 lambs are reared annually. The herbage of the South Downs, it is understood, consists principally of wild thyme, burnet, yarrow, trefoil, and eyebright. On these Downs the rams are turned into the flocks late in October or early in November, the lambs suck the ewes nearly four months before they are weaned, after which they are kept on rape, tares, or clover, and nothing better than clover."

To get back once more to Ellman's sheep, Arthur Young continues:

> "In a discourse on sheep, Mr. Ellman remarked, Brighton butchers sold legs and loins of mutton at 6d. per pound, necks at $5\frac{1}{2}$d., and breasts at only $3\frac{1}{2}$d., which, he observed, was a proof that the lighter a sheep was in his fore in proportion to his hind quarter, so much the better, that Mr. Ellman's Southdown wethers are 4 lbs. heavier in the hind quarter than they are in the fore, but at Mr. Coke's, at Holkham, a Bakewell wether, $3\frac{1}{2}$ years old, weighed 10 lbs.

heavier in the fore quarter than it did in the hind quarter.

"Mr. Ellman's flock of sheep, I must observe, is unquestionably the first in the country. There is nothing that can be compared with it, the wool the finest, and the carcase, the best proportioned, although I saw several of the noblest flocks afterwards, which I examined with a great degree of attention, some few had very fine wool which might be equal to his, but then, the carcase was ill-shaped, and many had a good carcase with coarse wool. But Ellman united both these circumstances in his flock at Glynde. The Southdown sheep is sufficiently domesticated for hill sheep, a breed which require but little activity to fill themselves on hard and short keep, between the hours of turning them out of the fold in the morning and putting them into it at night, a practice very general through the country. Mr. Ellman feeds usually about 100 wethers every year, and he sold them last year (1793) at 2½ years old for 36s. When weighed, they amounted to 21 lbs. to the quarter. The mutton is allowed to be equal to the best in the Island, and the average weight of their fleece varies from 2 to 2½ lbs. Mr. Ellman has clipped, when washed, more than 5 lbs. per fleece from several of his own breed, the highest price at which it sold, and which his wool fetched in 1792, was 2s. per lb. A common time of lambing the store ewes is the latter end of March, or beginning of April, and they are well-woolled at the time of lambing. No other breed is more healthy and hardy than this, and from the closeness of the wool they are well defended against the beating winds and rain, and they naturally possess a good constitution."

As a matter of interest to Sussex farmers of all generations, no history of their county breed would be complete without placing on record the opinion of Mr. Matthews, the Secretary of the Bath and West Show, in 1798, on the Sussex Agricultural Association, at Lewes, and referred to in Mr. F. P. Walesby's *Memoir*.

Mr. Matthews wrote:

"The increasing zeal of the Sussex farmers for improving by selection and care their native and invaluable breed of sheep, cannot be too much applauded. This spirit was displayed on a large scale in the most liberal manner, at the summer exhibition at Lewes, in 1798. . . . To see thirty or forty farmers bring forth each ten picked ewes of the same age from his flock, and place them in open pens side by side in a long rank, for the whole country to compare and improve by, while the premiums seemed to be an inferior object, and at the same time exhibiting for premium and sale some of the finest rams in the country, was no common occurrence. The landlords and chief gentlemen of the district mingling with those farmers encouraged them in their useful emulation, and taking a part with them in rural and peaceful contest were circumstances of additional pleasure."

During the heyday of Ellman's fame was instituted Selmiston Sheep Fair, of which the great flockmaster writes to Arthur Young, as follows:

"At Selmiston Fair yesterday, 19th September, 1793, we had a larger show of sheep and lambs than usual, about 8000. Do not remember ever having seen so few buyers, believe not more than a quarter sold, and those at reduced prices. Ewes from the Downs fetched from 18s. to 25s. Some small parcels from the Weald sold from 13s. to 17s., wethers from 20s. to 25s. head, wether lambs from 12s. to 15s. 6d.,

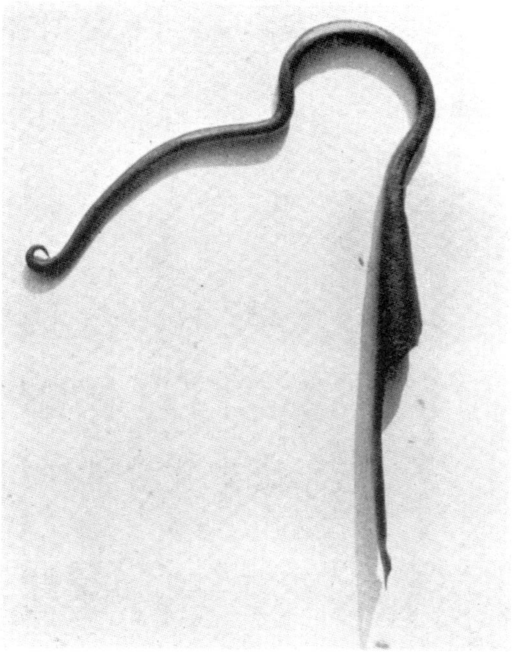

LAMBING-HOOK

TOM WRATTEN USING A

*Photos by the Author*

*Photo by "Farmer & Stockbreeder"*

BERT LINKHORN AT WORK

refuse ditto from 7s. 7d. to 11s. Did not hear of any ewe lambs being sold. Mr. Davies, of Bedingham, got the best prices for ewes, and Sir Charles Goring, for wether lambs. Saw no buyers from Norfolk, Suffolk, or Essex, and but few from Kent."

Another Fair which made its appearance a little later was Toy Fair, and this is well described by Mr. J. A. Erridge in his *History of Brighthelmston*.

Says this authority :

" Without doubt the Toy Fair was the earliest people's festival. It was formerly held on the cliff, between Ship Street and Black Lion Street, but the town increasing and the Fair assuming a corresponding magnitude, Belle Vue field, whereupon now stands Regency Square, was its location. From thence it was transplanted to the Level, where, on the 4th of September, 1807, a Sheep Fair was first held, notification of the same having been in the *Brighton Herald* and in the *Weekly Journal* published in Lewes, as follows :

" ' The rapid strides which agriculture has made within the last ten years, in this country, and the extreme utility which has been the result of its present scientific mode of practice has commanded the attention and admiration not only of all England, but of all civilized Europe. To those who are interested in the purchase of any particular breed of stock it must be of extreme importance that their stock be genuine and uncontaminated.

" ' To fix, therefore, a spot where a pure, unmixed breed shall always be produced, and where the purchaser (who, perhaps, comes from a distance) shall be sure of unadulterated stock, appears to be a great desideratum. In no instance is it more so than in that useful and highly-productive animal, the South Down

Sheep. Those who possess this breed, true and genuine, have much reason to lament that at Fairs, where a great variety of sheep are brought to market, many are sold for South Down Sheep which have no pretension to be so called, and which afterwards, not answering the purpose of the buyers, bring unmerited disgrace on such as are really genuine. We, therefore, the undersigned breeders of pure South Down Sheep have come to a resolution to establish a fair, to be holden on Brighton Level, the 4th of September, 1807. And we pledge ourselves to bring to it genuine South Down Tups, Stock Ewes, Ewe Lambs, and Weather Lambs; and, moreover, we will not either ourselves introduce, or suffer to be introduced to this fair any but what shall be of genuine and true South Down Breed.'

(Here followed the signature of many well-known flockmasters).

"About 20,000 prime South Down Sheep of all denominations found a ready sale, buyers being plentiful. The next year the sheep fair was equally well attended; but, notwithstanding the most strenuous exertions of its promoters, it had but an existence of four years."

Southdowns can withstand extremes of heat and cold, and will flourish in any climate, so long as it is moderately dry. Excessive wet underfoot they do not like, and this is only a natural feature, for they are bred and reared for the most part on chalky uplands, although they have become great favourites with farmers using farms on the low-lying arable land of the coast, and North of the South Downs

To quote once again from Ellman:

"Southdown sheep having been first cultivated and afterwards improved upon very thin land, consequently it proves them to be well adapted for poor soils, their hardy constitution fits them for difficult situations, and for the cultivation of poor soils, their activity resembles the hare, and points to the mountain as their home. Their wool being closely fitted to their backs (being tight and firm, resisting wet and cold) makes them well adapted to cold climates."

It is so well known a fact as hardly to bear repetition, that three Southdowns can be kept on food which would only suffice for two sheep of the larger breeds, and they are free from foot-rot, while as even dressers of the land they have no equal.

To realize the true value of the breed, one has to see them in their own native surroundings, whether grazing the short, sweet herbage of the Downs or feeding off roots and forage crops in their folds, and Southdowns are beautiful sheep to look at, and when one adds to this the remarkable manner in which their fold-tail benefits the ensuing crops, making possible the cultivation of land which would otherwise revert to grass, or become derelict, then one realizes they are the tenant farmers' sheep *par excellence*.

Mr. John Ellman always stated that it was more difficult to maintain a good breed than to raise it to first class, and therefore it speaks volumes for those who followed after that the Southdown now stands so pre-eminent amongst the breeds of sheep.

Like all pioneers, Ellman and Webb had their critics, but at their death, these critics stood defeated by the legacy left to agriculture, viz. that of the greatest breed of short-woolled sheep this country possesses.

*So greatly has posterity vindicated the judgment of these two great breeders that one finds SOUTHDOWN BLOOD in all, or nearly all, our present-day Down breeds of sheep.*

*It is doubtless on account of their ancient lineage that South-*

*down rams are so pre-potent. It is this power to transmit its own good qualities to its progeny which makes the Southdown so popular a sire for crossing on or grading up " Native or Unimproved breeds of sheep."*[1]

In reply to my enquiry regarding Sussex flocks, other than Southdowns, Mr. Walford Lloyd wrote :

" All Merinos are now extinct, and never held much place. Wiltshire Horns, and Dorset Horns, too, have gone. To-day there are some few flocks of Hampshire Downs (in the West) and Dorset Downs. In the East, around Hastings, Rye, and Battle there are some 'Kents' or Romney Marsh. There are also many 'flying' flocks of Cheviots (or the Scottish half-bred ewes) mated with Down rams, a few Exmoors, and a few Clun Forest (Wales) and Kerry Hill (Wales) ewes —most of these ewes mated with Southdown rams."

In connection with the remarkable prepotency of the Southdown breed a note which Mr. Ballantine discovered in *Chambers' Information for the People* for 1842 is worth recording :

" In a note to the author from Lord Pitnilly, near St. Andrews, are the following facts *re* Southdown sheep there : '. . . The lambs dropped early in winter 1839–1840 ; not being wanted were sent to Edinburgh. Ten of the ewes lambed again in September, 1840, and again in March, 1841.' "

Among my own notes of visits to shepherds I have the following item : At Pyecombe Walter Wooler showed me a Southdown ewe with four lambs, two of which were born on 26th July, 1929, and two born on 27th February, 1930, an interval of only seven months.

[1] Reprinted by permission of the author (E. Walford Lloyd, Esq.).

He also had another ewe which had one lamb born on 20th May, 1929, and two more on 1st February, 1930. It was unlucky that I had just used the last of my camera-film before I was shown the family in the pen.

The reduction in the number and size of Sussex flocks, compared with those of old days, is a matter for regret. Many people fail to understand the reason for the change. Like a certain old shepherd, whose opinion is recorded in a later chapter, they think that because sheep eat no more than their ancestors, and because their wool still grows the same as ever, that sheep-farming should pay.

The great decrease is probably due to a combination of circumstances and not to any one special reason. The vast amount of imported meat is doubtless the principal factor. Changes in hill-flocks followed the gradual passing away of old-fashioned Sussex farmers, whose thousands of sheep once found ample room on the Downs. The end of the old days, when a head shepherd ranked as a man of importance on a farm and was allowed his own way, saw the beginning of the decline in hill-flocks. Wonderful Downland farms deteriorated under new owners as local conditions were ignored and new methods adopted. It is found that farm flocks come to maturity quicker than those fed on the hills, and it has become necessary to take advantage of any method which will reduce costs, as a set-off against the many increased expenses forced upon flockmasters, in common with everyone else, by foreign competition and the changes which have followed the modern craze for speed in transit. There is no time now for old ways such as the old-fashioned men knew. Fewer flocks are driven over the hills; fewer still along the roads. Motor transport compels shepherds to keep time with other people in whom they have no interest. They tell you, too, the farmers are always " poking round " and giving instructions, while on some farms a man is expected to do other work in addition to acting as shepherd. Time-saving and competition have swept away all the romance attached to sheep-farming and have made it a cut business ; and so, as the oldest shepherds pass away, we are quickly losing the last links with peaceful prosperous days which will never return.

In addition to the old men who link us with other days and ways there are many more shepherds still in the prime of life. Some of these are just as intolerant of modern conditions as their elders, and will doubtless break away from what they know to be a thankless task. Others, who have inherited that strange passion for sheep which runs through some families, will possibly carry on under any sort of conditions. A proportion of them are already little more than " hurdle pitchers," as the old men term them, because they are not allowed to do or to know what is best for the flock.

It is strange that while modern changes have had such an effect on some men the great progress of Southdown show flocks has enabled others to find an outlet for their inborn love for work among sheep. Without the hearty co-operation of the shepherds who rear and prepare animals for the show-pens such results as we see could not be achieved, and although any one of these shepherds may feel, in his heart, that he is not in the position his father was, or his grandfather was, and that he has been caught in the web of modern ways, he is aware that such work as he is doing also shows the pride in personal effort which was a secret delight to his ancestors.

Mr. Walford Lloyd wrote to me as follows :

> " In your work on Sussex shepherds I feel that it would be incomplete unless you included a few notes on the greatest of our modern South Down shepherds,

Bert Linkhorn, who is shepherd to Mr. John Langmead, of Northwood, Ford, Arundel."

I found Mr. Linkhorn at his home at Clymping, where he entertained me with many interesting comments on his favourite Southdowns and the many matters connected with them.

It is seldom that one meets so modest a man as Bert Linkhorn, but my enthusiasm for the subject tempted him to speak freely about shows, prize-winners, modern shepherds and much more, and to produce many photographs for my inspection. He comes from a family of Hampshire shepherds. He was formerly at Goodwood, where he gained many awards, and since he came to Mr. Langmead many further successes have rewarded him for his untiring efforts.

As we chatted about the older shepherds he expressed the opinion that although some of their little ways and details connected with the care of sheep must continue, and cannot be improved upon, the extreme, business-like methods employed to-day to rear the wonderful prize-winners must inevitably replace most of the old customs and tend to produce more modern shepherds of his own type. His son is following on in the same line.

I gathered the impression that Mr. Linkhorn was not exactly anxious to be considered anything else than a shepherd; and certainly not as an extraordinary man with magic power over sheep. His love for sheep is inherited, and his years with the Goodwood and Ford flocks have caused him to specialize in the work connected with show-pens. Photographs, papers, letters, and cards shower down upon him, but he is not spoilt by all the attention he receives. He is a worker. "I could talk sheep to you till the cows come home," he said, with a smile, "but I must be on the move now! You shall see more if you care to come along to the barn."

As we walked along the shepherd said: "I have a nice crook that was handed down to me. It is over a hundred years old. You shall see it." And when we reached the barn he produced it. It was made in Hampshire and is a very beautiful crook now in spite of its age. I learned that it once had a fancy scalloped edge on the barrel, but unfortunately this has been filed off. In its original state the crook must have been an unusually beautiful specimen of smith's work.

Assistants were busy preparing sheep for Mr. Linkhorn to trim. He donned his apron and commenced work with the shears. "We use other things here besides the usual old brush and shears," he explained. "Naturally I have little ways of my own in turning out sheep fit to show. Sometimes I have letters asking what I do and what I use. I can't answer such questions—how can I? People shouldn't expect to be told all those things in a letter! I do the work in my own way, and the cards keep on going up there!" I looked up. High above the pens big boards held rows and rows of prize-winners' cards which record the successes of the Ford flock—fifty-odd on one, ninety on another, and so on—a bewildering show! I gasped as I saw them. "We have started again this year," said the shepherd, as he extracted another pile from a big box—"these are from two shows!"

I watched this modern shepherd at his work as he used tools that were new to me and then clipped with the shears. He showed me how it was possible, by deft clipping, to accentuate the good points of a sheep, although, as he remarked: "You can't expect to win by clipping if there isn't something good under the wool when the judge's fingers touch it!" One had to glance at the one animal being scrubbed and then at the one on which he was working, to appreciate the shepherd's ability.

I have watched a famous artist paint a sketch of a bird, with a colour-charged sable brush without any previous outline. I have seen him use a favourite old worn brush to obtain a magic effect of broken tints. I have seen a wood-carver make the first cuts on a panel in an apparently careless way which left me breathless.

In the old barn at Clymping I watched Bert Linkhorn use his shears on a beautiful, valuable animal and transform it with the same sure touch of a master-hand.

A picture may be hung; a carving may be exhibited; a pen of sheep which win a trophy for the farmer may bring the shepherd money and a cardboard ticket, but artist, carver, and shepherd have already obtained something which cannot be purchased—the secret joy in completion of work with which their hearts are in tune.

The old men grumble, and tell me that the days of pride in work are over for ever, but my visit to Clymping proved that, like a spark among cinders, pride in the shepherd's work still survives, ready to kindle afresh if opportunity is given.

---

The following article by Mr. John Langmead, owner of the famous Ford flock, reveals the completeness of the methods adopted by which the sheep under Bert Linkhorn's charge are brought to perfection. Although it was published some years ago, its information and interest is as fresh as ever, and it is reprinted here by kind permission of the Author, and the Editor of the *Farmer and Stockbreeder*.

### Getting the Smithfield Type

#### By JOHN LANGMEAD

Many no doubt suspect that winning at shows is largely the result of high feeding and the skilful use of the shears. The experienced flockmaster knows, of course, that nothing could be farther from the truth. The dangers of continuous and heavy feeding of concentrates are well known. A forcing diet over a short period is equally likely to defeat the object in view.

To some it may be a surprise that even for concentrates we depend entirely on home-grown stuffs, whether in feeding for Smithfield or the summer shows, or in ordinary flock routine. Three parts crushed oats (a good, safe sheep food), one of bean meal, and one of ground linseed (grown on the farm and ground by mixing a few oats with it), is the standard mixture for ewes suckling twins, for weaned lambs, as well as for show sheep.

*Feeding for Show.*

Even for Smithfield, no sheep has more than 1lb. a day of this concentrate mixture. The exact feeding programme for our Smithfield sheep is at 7 a.m. about half a pound of the concentrate mixture, followed by a bushel of cut swedes between six. At midday they get half a cabbage apiece, and at 4.30 p.m. the second half of the concentrates ration and roots. Last thing in the evening they have a handful of hay, preferably made from Dutch clover. The quantities in question are hardly an accurate guide as to amounts that would be required in the case of bigger breeds, for the Southdown is naturally a small eater.

Undoubtedly, the chief point in show feeding is constant care and attention. What they have they have regularly, day in, day out, and at regular hours. In regard to the more immediate preparation for show or sale, it should be said straightaway that nothing that can be done with the shears will make an indifferent sheep into a good one. The good points and uniformity in fleshing can be made to appeal more to the eye, but it is impossible to conceal faults from a judge who knows his work. A hindquarter can be trimmed to show what *appears* to be a good leg of mutton, but the judge's fingers will sink into the wool the moment he lays his hand on the weak place.

Before any sheep can be fed and trimmed for successful showing, one cannot too over-emphasize the necessity for the right material to work on. In addition to the capacity for uniform fleshing and general symmetry of a finished Smithfield animal, the sheep must possess a fair measure of the all-round character that is the primary aim of a pedigree breeder: the long, wide, deep body carried close to the ground on legs well put on in line with the outside of the body; the even top line, finishing in a wide dock reasonably level with the backbone; the well-filled leg of mutton; the bold head neatly carried on a short neck, with ears set wide apart. All these points are essentially a question of breeding.

*Selection of the Raw Material.*

To have the best material to work on, one must have a reasonable number of sheep of sufficient merit from which to choose. In the Ford flock (I need not concern myself here with the Flamsham and the Bognor Regis flocks at the moment), I have reckoned on keeping forty or fifty of the best ram lambs for sale as breeding stock; the remaining fifty or so male sheep are cut, and are, of course, available as wether lambs or wether sheep for fat-stock show purposes.

They include some, no doubt, superior to hundreds of rams used in good commercial flocks. On the other hand, certain characteristics important in a breeding animal are not of great significance in a fat-stock show animal. A sheep may stand a little too high from the ground to stand a chance at the Royal, and yet be an excellent entry for Smithfield if it has sufficient merit otherwise. Quality of wool has always been a guiding factor, and it may be taken that a good, close-textured wool, soft to the touch, resistant to weather, and filling the hand at a grasp, generally covers a well-meated body.

In the case of a pedigree flock, and particularly, as in our case, where every ewe is individually recorded and the pedigree of every lamb is available at a moment's notice, we are, perhaps, at some advantage in making a selection for any particular purpose in comparison with the owner of a commercial flock. One can tell at as early as six weeks of age what a lamb is going to make by the way it is shaping and the stock it is bred from. What has been bred in must come out.

In this connection one cannot but deprecate the practice of many commercial breeders of continually changing the type of ram used. The drawbacks of using different types from year to year are far greater than any conceivable dangers of close-breeding through going consistently to one flock for one's change of blood. When a man finds the blood from a certain flock suits his purpose, let him stick to it—provided only that the ram breeder himself is duly changing *his* blood.

*Housing for Show.*

We reckon to bring the sheep intended either for showing at Smithfield or at shows the following summer into the barn about the end of September. Up to that point they will possibly have been on clover gratton, preferably white clover, trefoil or kale, and getting about $\frac{1}{2}$lb. of concentrates in the case of wethers for Smithfield and $\frac{3}{4}$lb. in the case of the ram lambs for the autumn sales. The Ford flock, it should be explained, has always been an arable-land, folding flock—although the Southdown adapts itself so well to grazing.

Between early October and the Smithfield Show, my

shepherd will count on going over the show sheep at least three times with the shears, at intervals of three or four weeks. The first trim he will take fairly freely of the loose ends, getting more or less down to the compact part of the fleece, bearing in mind that one can always take a little more off, but that what is off cannot be replaced. Also, he has to make sure that any sheep to be shown in one pen are nicely matched up. The top line, of course, receives special attention at this first trimming, for it is undesirable that the wool shall present the freshly pared-down look always so unsightly.

Exercise is important, whether in sheep being prepared for show or in breeding stock. The Smithfield sheep in the barn, for example, are walked out every morning for possibly half a mile, the wether sheep going out twice a day. To do themselves justice in the ring, standing and walking with reasonable ease, it is essential that they be kept thoroughly accustomed to their increasing weight, and I recall more than one championship lost on this account. This is, of course, apart from considerations in connection with the general health of the sheep. Breeding ewes, for instance, I like to do something like two miles a day.

*The Final Trim.*

A week or two before the show, the shepherd will do his final trimming, this time removing as little wool as possible. These finishing touches would be difficult to do successfully had the preliminary work not been correctly carried out. The aim, of course, is to bring out all the good points of the sheep and to emphasize the uniformity and even fleshing without achieving exaggerated effects. Only patience, skill, and an eye for a good sheep can achieve the result which denotes the master hand. The trimming completed, a light dressing with ochre (as little as possible) affords nicely matched and even colouring throughout the pen.

There is no disputing that these final preparations do enhance the appearance of a sheep, even to the trained eye. At the same time, I would emphasize that unless the sheep is there to start with, the trimming may be worse than useless and only have the result of making the faults all the more noticeable when the animal is handled. Although the sheep is no better or no worse for this final preparation, it undoubtedly facilitates judging by showing up immediately the sheep combining character, symmetry, and even fleshing from those lacking in even one of these respects.

## THE CROW-SCARER

I HAD arranged to meet Shepherd X to receive an old shears-pouch which he had promised to give me. After waiting some time in the cold north-east wind I sheltered behind a thick hedge,—"in the loo," as shepherds say,—and was soon interested in the movements of a wren, which appeared from the tangle of sticks and ivy at the root of a bush near me.

The sudden sound of a gunshot on the far side of the field caused many alarmed rooks to rise in a confused crowd and scatter in all directions. Even where I stood the report caused a commotion among finches and blackbirds, and revealed the presence of two redwings, which hurried away.

Soon a little figure appeared, far away on the field. It was Shepherd X, armed with a gun instead of a crook, and I walked towards him.

"Scarin' rooks I be, now," he said, as we met, "but they jus' be artful! I diddun get one, tho' I bin waitin' o'er yonder 'bout three-quarters-hour! Now I be off o'er t' hill;—there be wheat set there, too."

As we trudged, with bent heads, up the hill and over the brow he explained why he carried a gun. "I be s'posed not to mind work Sundays," he said "'cos I was shepherd, an' used to it. Some of us beant shepherds now, you know. Farmers be t' shepherds now, but *we* still doos t' work! Why, when I worked for Mus Brown *he* wur t' *farmer*, an' *I* wur t' *shepherd*. He grew t' food I wanted, an' bought what else I asked him for, an' t' sheep paid very well. *Now* I don' know *what* I be! This year I helped wi' t' lambin'; in middle of it I wur fetched 'way to be carter fur three weeks, then back to t' sheep agen, then in t' turnip field, then summat else. Boss be allus pokin' I 'bout, first one place, then 'nother, an' when I spoke to he 'bout it he said if *I* wurn't here he mus' have a steward, an' there be nowheres for steward but t' farmhouse, an' he don' want un there, so now I be telled what's t' be done, an' I see *'tis* done, an' yet I be crow-scarer or summat else Sundays! Well, a job ain't so easy got now-days, so I goos on an' on an' say nothen. Times I know Boss be wrong, an' I thinks ' All right, you get on wi' it!' "

Over the brow I stopped to look at the shears-pouch, —a perfect specimen and carefully preserved in spite of its age. " I've no use much now for shears," said X,— " I've got one pair as never done any work at all, but when I really wur a shepherd I wur allus trimmin', sometimes six weeks at a time. Now-days lots don' trim at all, or if they doos they jus cuts the tails square an' makes 'em clean an' tidy. Thet ain't trimmin', but 'tis good 'nough fur these days!"

As we approached the big field he was watching carefully, but no rooks were to be seen. Our movements scared some pigeons. " I got a nice pigeon last week," he remarked, " he made a tasty meal." Suddenly he said: " I really mus' try an' knock over one o' they rooks, though I don't know as I care 'bout t' job.— Boss, he spects t' see one or two dead uns' hanged up in his fields, but some'ow I likes rooks flyin',—they be good ol' weather-prophets when rain be comin'. I knows they be mischiful varmints in t' cornfield, but when I wur young a boy wur kep' as crow-scarer. Boss wunt pay boy to scare 'em,—sends *me* out Sundays to *shoot* 'em!—so if I can I scares 'em by shootin' sumthin' I can eat!"

## THE CROW-SCARER 241

I left him in the hedge, with his gun in his hand, and doddled homewards with the precious pouch. The way was full of delightful scenes, as usual—the avenue through a covert, filled with brilliant yellow splashes of field maple and masses of hazel leaves, clumps of dead bracken and bits of crimson and yellow on the brambles. A cock pheasant strutted across the muddy path as I left the avenue. On the big Downland field of plaintain, cropped low by sheep, was a flock of peewits and a few partridges, and as I came nearer to home I passed some tall elms, still thinly dressed in yellow leaves. On the topmost branches several rooks were resting, their dark plumage shining like silk, and I thought of the match of wits between bird and man for possession of grains of corn. As I stood to enjoy the picture—blue sky, yellow leaves and big glossy black birds—my sympathy was with the rooks. I hoped they would be too "artful" for the shepherd, or anyone else with a gun. Sussex landscapes would be much less attractive without the dear old rooks and their familiar harsh call!

## AN OLD SHEPHERD'S OPINION

I WAS fortunate to catch old John when he had just finished folding on a Sunday afternoon and was in the mood for a chat. I wanted to hear his views on show flocks, but at the mere mention of them his face expressed disdain. "Show flocks be all very well in their way," he remarked, "but they beant worth all the money spent on 'em. I don't think much to 'em myself, as they be to-day!" At his leisure, and in his own peculiar way, he expressed the opinion that, to his idea, the show business is carried to extremes. "Of course," he explained, "'tis only like lots of other things that we don't really want so much of, but 'tis the fashion, an' so we haves it."

John lit his pipe and continued: "I know I only have a hill flock," he said, "but I know what I'm talkin' 'bout, an' I know none o' mine would be any good for show 'gainst a farm flock (they be too long in the leg for one thing), but when I wur a boy of *nine* I helped my father to trim sheep! Why! do you know that I wur on'y high 'nough at nine to stand an' clip a sheep's back? My father stood by me doing another, an' it diddun pay me to make a wrong cut. If I did he saw it, an' down came his hard hat on me with a heavy smack! I wur *made* to learn, an' in the end I wur as good as he." Presently he remarked: "Perhaps you won't believe it, but I could stand beside the best of 'em wi' a pair o' shears an' a brush, even now, if I had a good sheep to work on!"

I ventured to remind him of the fact that no clipping can transform a poor sheep into a good one. "Why! of course they say so to-day," he replied, "'cause 'tis business. If people sells fish they don't ever say it stinks,—do 'em? They say how good it be! 'Tis the same with everything now, but when I was nine!"——— He paused again to put another match to his clay pipe, and I settled myself on the top step of his hut—"Now you knows me, an' I knows you!" he said, "an' I shouldn' sit here wastin' my time an' yours a'tellin' stories;—now I'm going to tell you something. When I wur a boy my father had a flock of four hundred. You could go among that lot an' see all the faces alike,— all a pretty grey mousey colour, an' ne'er a bit o' wool on one of the faces. An' all their legs wur nice an' short wid little thin bones, an' their coats was a picture. You'd have a job to find a flock of four hundred like that to-day! Now, the best of a flock like that wur good sheep to work on,—there warn't anything that wanted hiding, an' when we had finished them off by trimming they wur worth showing!"

The shepherd's mate appeared and asked if there was anything more to do. "No," said John,—"you goo off,—I'll give a look round afore I goo." And then he resumed: "Take rams, now, I wouldn' goo fur to buy one o' they show rams. I'd rather have mine in the rough, an' a lean one at that. Then I *would* know what I was buying, an' what sort of lambs to expect. I remember ol' Mus B——— (I was his shepherd then). He bought a big ram at a auction sale an' sent it home. I thought he knew better! I could trim a ram with the best of 'em, an' I knows what to look for;—some places his wool was quite short an' in others 'twas thick. He'd bin nicely trimmed an' finished off to hide up what wanted hiding. Nex' day the ol' man says to me: "What d'ye think o' the new ram, Shepherd?" I said:

"I don't like him at all." "Oh," he says, quick, "but I paid forty-five guineas for him!" "I don't care nothen 'bout that," I says, " if I thinks a thing I says it;— you wait till he's sheared nex' year an' you'll see he's a ugly ol' devil! He was fair upset when I told him the rights of it!"

"I remember," continued John, "I once went with father to a sale to get a ram. At last we found a likely looking one. He handled it all over, and everybody was surprised when he refused it. 'It won't do for me,' he said, and walked off. He had found a lot of knots in the wool. Oh, yes! he was a very particular man;—*he* knew how to buy a ram!"

Once more the shepherd lighted up. I did not interrupt, and he soon started again. "Lor bless me!" he burst out, "I'll tell you now jus' what 'tis. When I was a young man the shepherd was the shepherd an' the farmer was the farmer, an' each kep' his place. Boss 'd say, at the sales, 'Pick out what you want, shepherd, an' we'll have it.' I took that pride in my flock as if 'twas my own, an' when show time came round I wur ready for it. Nowadays farmers wants to be shepherds as well half the time, an' when that happens the shepherd loses interest, and only waits for Saturday night for his pay. 'Tis a pity 'tis so, but '*tis* so,—an' there 'tis! I know the feeling myself, yet I still go on, an' get a prize now an' then,—why?—because 'tis inside me, I suppose, for I do *hate* to see a poor-looking lot of sheep!— But all I do," he added, "is done in the old-fashioned way, with just a brush an' shears, an' you can't beat it! Now some uses a wire dabber thing. I was given one, but I put the damn thing on the fire. I can do better with a good scrubbing brush, for I be used to it!"

I might have heard more, but visitors broke the spell, and old John started up in alarm. "Damn the people coming roun' the fold," he muttered, "they'll spile that dog o' mine!" He ordered the shaggy dog to lie down, he told a surprised girl to go away, and waited till she did so. Then he turned back to me. "Come an' see the bes' ewes I've picked out for the boss," he said, "an' then I mus goo, for I bin sitting there, an' 'tis four o'clock, an' I arn't bin home to dinner!"

# THE END OF THE BOOK

"I BE 'bout done!" the old man said,
   "I can't do much work now;—
I reckon this ol' crook'll las'
   My time out any'ow!
'Twas my son's crook afore 'e died,
   An' since 'e's gone, yew see
I likes to carry it 'bout
   To kip me company!"


"When ol' John Barley 'ad t' farm
   I liked t' work fur 'e;—
'E wur a proper farmer, an'
   'E lef' t' sheep t' me,
But since a sheereman took it on,
   (Which aren't so very long)
T' ol' place beänt like t' same
   An' everythin' be wrong!"


"I reckon I'll be glad t' stop
   A-workin' fur a man
Like *this 'un* is!—yew beänt right
   Tho' yew doos all yew can!
They all allows as this ol' farm's
   A good un!—on t' west
We've allus growed t' corn an' stuff

Becos thet ground's t' best,
An' all thet big bit on t' east
Is on'y grazin' ground,—
Then why not let t' ol farm bide
As 'twas ?—*'E changed it round !*
'E ploughed up all t' grass this year,
An' said 'twur right fur corn !—
I never see sich gooin's on
Since ever I wur born !
'E 'urries 'ere, an' urries there,—
An' now 'e'll 'urry more,
Fur now 'e wants it all putt back
Jus' like 'twas afore ! "

" T' times 'ere be too fas' fur me !—
Yew know t' Bible sayes
T' 'eavens an' earth an' everythin'
Wur all made in six days ?—
Well,—thet wur quick 'nough sure-ly !
But still thet wouldn' do
Fur *this un*, cos 'e'd want t' lot
All done fur *'im* in *two !* "

Most of the lines above are the actual words of a certain old shepherd. As I wrote the account of my interview with him in my note-book many of his sentences threaded themselves together and rhymed. His statements and comments were made with such precision that he must have pondered long on the uncomfortable state of things of which he spoke while he minded his small flock of tegs, and his thoughts must have arranged themselves in rhyme in his mind. Old Jim never talks at random ;—his words are always impressive and his ideas are clearly expressed, and one feels that his complaints are not those of an ordinary grumbler, because there is more sadness than bitterness in his voice when comparing past days with the present.

Some of the old men do not express their opinions so mildly. I heard one giving vent to his feelings as he conversed with a friend at Findon Fair. "Farmers don' want shepherds now, Jack," he said, vigorously; "all they wants is hurdle-pitchers an' drovers ! The shepherd beant *supposed* to know anythin'.—Farmer knows,— an' if he don' know 'e *thinks* 'e doos, an 'e says what's t' be done. Lord bless us ! why, I wouldn't a-had thet when *I* wur shepherd !—Damn ! I'd a-walked off,— an' so'd yew, reckon?" His friend agreed, and he continued : "Look at some of 'em 'ere t'day ; dressed up wid tassels on their stockin's !—walkin' round' an' feelin' t' sheep an' lambs 's if they knows all there be *to* know ! I wonder 'ow they'd goo on if they 'ad some o' t' jobs as *us* 'as 'ad, eh, Jack?—Reckon they'd be callin' out fur t' ol' shepherd, quick !"

Such little grumbles are the privilege of the aged, and are merely incidental to comparison of present conditions with ways which will never return. In vain you may point out that farmers you know are better than many other people. The old men do not seem to realize that times have changed for farmers as well as for themselves. They are naturally impatient as they see methodical habits of a lifetime superseded by new ideas, but due allowance must be made for their point of view. It must be sad indeed for them to reflect on the fact that although they were once important men their power has now crumbled away and that they are members of a dying race.

Those who care to seek the last of the old shepherds will be well entertained. They will be able to verify such details as are recorded here, to gather fresh facts, to obtain fresh pictures, and to enjoy the beauty, romance, quaintness, and humour which is the reward of the enthusiast. The opportunity will soon pass. The old type of shepherd will soon fade out, and the poetry and romance of the shepherd's life will pass away with them, for there will be little to record in accounts of future shepherds of Sussex!

# INDEX

## A

Archæological facts regarding sheep, 30

## B

Bailey, George, 82
Beckett, Arthur, 38, 47, 193
Beecher, John, 183
Bells, 19, 55, 60, 92, 133
Berry, Crookmaker, Pyecombe, 79
Black lambs, 193
Blackmore, Stephen, 46
Blackpatch Hill, 33, 35
Blann, Michael, 62, 207
Brass Crooks, 127
"Break'em in young!" 200
Brown, John (West Blatchington), 77
Browne and Crosskey (Lewes), 124
Bustards on Sussex Downs, 46

## C

Canary Islands, natives of, 31
Coppard, Nelson, 16, 54
Corncrake's call, 186
Cow in lambing-fold, 95
Cox, Jack, 59
Crooks (or hooks), 39, 59, 69, 73, 79, 126, 190, 232
Cure by odour from sheep, 185

## D

"Damn," and its meanings, 196
Dawkins, Sir Wm. Boyd, 30
Decrease in Sussex flocks, 229
Dew-ponds, 176
Dipping hook, 56, 113, 170
Dogs, 39, 57, 82, 91, 178, 180
Dudeney, John, 43
Duly, William, 80

## INDEX

### E

Early Iron Age, 33
*Early Man in Britain*, 30
East Dean, 38, 80
East Guldeford, 210
Elderberry lotion, 72, 212
Ellman, John, 41, 216

### F

Falmer crook, 130
" Farthing-in-the-ear " mark, 172
Fat-tailed sheep, 194
Fern bedding for huts, 32
Findon Fair, 63
Findon Park, 33
Flint axes, 188
Flint mines, 33
*Flint Miners of Blackpatch*, 35
Fowler, Jim, 101
Freak lambs, 100
Frost, Miss M., 38
Fulking, 168
Funeral customs, 99, 195
Funnell, Darkie, 103

### G

Gerard, Miss E., 38
Godden, Tom, 209
*Government of Cattel* (1596), 38
Guanchos, the, 32

### H

Harrow Hill, 33, 60
Hemming, Mr. and Mrs., 47
Herbs, 71
Hill-shepherd, 19, 24
Horn cups, 157
Horn lanterns, 65, 117
Humphrey, George, 70

### J

Jaw bone of prehistoric sheep, 34
Johnson, Walter, 53

### K

Kingston by Lewes, 45
Kingston crooks, 129

### L

Lamb jackets, 56, 102
Lambing-hooks, 209, 210
Langmead, John, 233
Lee Farm, 59
Linkhorn, Bert, 231
Lower, Richard, 42

# INDEX

## M

*Magpie House*, 47
Marking irons, 68, 70, 111
Mascal, Leonard (1596), 38
*Men of the Old Stone Age*, 31
Merry Shepherd, the, 165
Mist on the hills, 181
Mitchell, Charles, 69
Mixed flocks, 40
Moulding, Jesse, 73

## N

Neolithic shepherds, 31
Neolithic shepherds (links with), 32
Newell, Shepherd, 183
Newmarket Hill, 45
Norris, John, 120, 191
Nutley, Ted, 55, 188

## O

Old Sussex farmers, 77, 81
Oxen (records of), 58, 79

## P

Parsons, Fred (Alfriston), 206
Plumpton, 44

Prepotency of Southdown sheep, 228
Pull, John H., 34
Pyecombe hooks, 39, 59, 129

## R

Rabbits and hares, 189
Reed-flute, 32
Rewell, Henry, 102
Robinson, Miss Maude, 157
Roller wattles, 201
Rottingdean, 45
Rough characters on downs, 75, 189, 192
Rusbridge, Tom, 98, 122
Rye, 208

## S

Saddlescombe Farm, 157
Sainsbury, C. H., 34
Saint's handbell, 136
Shearing gangs, 83, 154, 159, 211
Shears pouch, 84, 110, 239
Sheep bows, 110
  counting, 174
  diseases, 69
  dogs, 57
  fairs, 76, 78, 83, 224, 225
  jaws from excavation, 34
  marking, 56, 67, 70, 73, 172
  pens, 38, 67

# INDEX

Sheep washing, 168
  of Swiss pile dwellings, 30
Shepherd, William, 192
Shepherd as crow-scarer, 239
Shepherds' "mess" of greens, 74
  complaints, 185
  clothes, 57, 60, 63, 69, 72, 81, 83, 121
  "crowns," 188
  huts, 40, 107
  music, 32, 64, 72, 206
  possessions, 17, 39, 107
  shelters, 31, 32, 69, 72, 205
  stools, 114
  sundials, 58, 203
  toast, 102
  umbrellas, 81, 83, 114, 125
  whistle-pipes, 65, 207
  wives assist in work, 43, 44, 60
Smuggling, 26, 37, 38, 50
Soutar, Andrew, 47
Southdown sheep, 213
Southdown Sheep Society, 213
*Spirit of the Downs*, 47
Stanmer Down Pond, 177
Stone-throwing by shepherds, 191
*Stray Leaves* (1862), 42
*Sussex Archæological Collections*, 37, 43
Sussex beer, 160, 193
Sussex character, 26
*Sussex County Magazine*, 15, 46, 146, 172
Sussex Fairs, 78, 83, 224, 225

Sussex hats, 123
*Sussex in Bygone Days*, 168
Sussex linen, 123
Sussex Marshes, 208

## T

Tackle for sheep-bells, 148
Tailing, 112
*Talks with Shepherds*, 53
Tar-boy, 156, 159
Tenantry flocks, 42
Thatching needles, 109
Toms, H. S., 177
Training of shepherds, 22
Trigwell, Charles, 73
Trigwell, Tom, 73

## U

Upton, Frank, 77

## V

Verneau, Dr. René, 31

## W

Walford Lloyd, H., 174, 214
Walker and Loach (makers of horn lanterns), 118

Wattles, old and new, 79, 192
West Blatchington, 45, 77
Wheatears, 45, 46, 101
Whisky for ewes, 194
White, Gilbert, 201, 215
Winchelsea, 209
Wool smuggling, 37
Wooler, Walter, 67
Worthing Museum, 18, 109, 120
Wratten, Ernest, 210